RAYMOND WILLIAMS:
FILM
TV
CULTURE

A publication accompanying a season

of films and television at the

National Film Theatre,

June, 1989

Edited by David Lusted

NFT/BFI Education

ALSO IN THIS SERIES

A BFI Education publication produced by the National Film Theatre, London, 1989.

British Library Cataloguing in Publication
Raymond Williams: Film TV Culture 1: Film and TV
I. Lusted, David

ISBN: 0-85170-248-1

Typeset by Kate Jennings, Wordprocessing, Desktop Publishing, Training and Consultancy.
Printed by the BFI.
Cover design by Julia King.
Stills courtesy of: Artificial Eye, BBC TV, Gaumont, William MacQuitty, Palace Pictures, Paramount Pictures Corporation, Rank Film Distributors, Weintraub Entertainment.
Cover printed and bound by Kent Paper Company Limited.

The British Film Institute, 21 Stephen Street, London W1P 1PL.

Acknowledgements

Thanks to Charlie Ritchie, Paul Allitt and Ryan Musgrove of Cambridge Alternative Video Group; BBC Archive; The Broadcasting and Entertainment Trades Alliance for financiaal assistance with the NFT season of films; Graham Martin, David Curry and Clare Duckmanton of the Open University; John Osmond and Colin Thomas of *The Divided Kingdom* series; Gwynn Pritchard and Heather Crowther of C4; Emyr Daniel of HTV; Mick Gold; *Undercut* Magazine; Mary Joannou; Gillian Swanson; Mark Atkin, Waltraud Loges, Rita Foreman and Sheila Whitaker of the NFT; Jayne Pilling of BFI Distribution; Gale Hamlin, Rachael Stroud, Julie Maher and colleagues in BFI Education; Wilf Stevenson, BFI Director; BFI Press Office staff. Special thanks to all contributors including, above all, Joy Williams.

Dedication

Raymond Williams 1921-1988

Notes on Contributors

Jim Cook works for the British Film Institute Education Department.

John Ellis is author of *Visible Fictions* (RKP 1982) and an independent producer with Large Door Ltd. who made *Raymond Williams — A Tribute* for C4 among documentaries on aspects of media and culture, including *Visions*.

Danielle Gardner is a postgraduate student in English Literature at Columbia University in New York, currently residing in London.

Noel King is one of Australia's leading film critics and teachers, currently in the Department of Humanities in the University of Technology, Sydney.

Alan Lovell, film critic and educationist, works for the Birmingham Film and Video Workshop.

David Lusted works for the British Film Institute Education Department.

Andy Medhurst is a freelance lecturer and journalist in film and television.

Francis Mulhern participated in the book-length interviews with Raymond Williams, *Politics and Letters: Interviews with New Left Review* (Verso, 1979).

Charlie Ritchie is a member of the Cambridge Alternative Video Group which made *DH Lawrence and the Culture Industry* and *Making Shakespeare*, both featuring Raymond Williams.

Raphael Samuel is an historian at Ruskin College and an editor of *History Workshop Journal*.

Dai Smith is a Professor in the School of History at the University of Wales, Cardiff and is working on the official biography of Raymond Williams.

Jenny Uglow is a writer (*The MacMillan Biographical Dictionary of Women*, 1989) and principal editor at The Hogarth Press, Chatto and Windus, who publish Williams's fiction, *Culture and Society* and *Towards 2000* among others.

Tana Wollen works for the British Film Institute Education Department.

Ken Worpole is a freelance writer and arts adviser, currently writing a book on cities and communications with Geoff Mulgan which draws upon Raymond Williams's work.

Joy Williams assisted in research for *The Long Revolution* and many other publications written by her husband, Raymond.

Table of Contents

Preface

David Lusted

I never knew anyone who had a deeper respect for rational enquiry than Raymond Williams, and that from a man who knew as well as anybody that reason is not, in the end, where it is at. He never underestimated the value of the intellectual tools of which his own people had been deliberately deprived; it was just that he took the instruments which he had been handed and turned them against the educators. He used them instead to create the finest body of cultural work of twentieth-century Britain, on behalf of those who had not enjoyed the privilege of arriving in Cambridge to be told by E.M.W. Tillyard that his boots were rather large. (Terry Eagleton, 'Resources for a Journey of Hope: The Significance of Raymond Williams', *New Left Review*, No. 168, March/April 1988.)

In his lifetime, Raymond Williams produced a remarkable body of writing and teaching. He wrote and taught about literature, drama and fiction; communications and culture; politics and social identity. He wrote in the forms of theory and criticism, his own fiction and drama; he wrote for and intervened in immediate cultural and political struggles as well as towards longer term understandings.

This publication offers an introduction to his ideas and ways of being, but it is most concerned with the legacy of his work, how it is to be maintained and carried on.

The focus is film and television, arenas that were merely a part of Williams's extensive interests. But the influence of his writing and teaching about film and television, both as products and institutions, was considerable. Generations of nascent film, TV and cultural critics, writers and academics met his ideas either directly, through his teaching in adult education, later as Professor of Drama at Cambridge, or indirectly through his writing. (No single books or articles represent the extent of his contribution but some of the key titles are listed for reference in the Select Bibliography.)

This publication was produced to accompany a season of films and television programmes screened at the National Film Theatre in June, 1989. It offers a novel approach to introducing and extending Williams's ideas. A broad range of cultural figures were invited to select and write about a film or television programme title for the season. Fifteen contributors write here about those selections, exploring the complex of intellectual and personal connections they draw from Williams's work. Some have an intimate knowledge of film or TV criticism, others are journalists or historians, still others produce on film or video. The contributions form an eclectic range of writing and see in Williams associations and possibilities that may surprise and challenge.

By marking Williams's life and work in this form, it is intended to acknowledge a huge debt to him but it also recognises a legacy of responsibility and commitment. The NFT and the BFI join with contributors to this publication in that recognition. The work of understanding and transformation goes on.

Introducing Raymond Williams

Francis Mulhern

Some years ago Raymond Williams gave a talk on the future of English studies. His audience was a group of Oxford students who, then as now, were engaged in a struggle to reform the deeply conservative programme and practice of the discipline at Oxford. He spoke of the new theoretical and historical challenges to settled syllabuses and settled ways of reading them, of the kinds of extension and reconstruction that were practicable and necessary. Probably not all that he said was quite welcome to his listeners — it was not his habit to encourage his audiences in their existing sense of the obvious. But his dominant note was one of solidarity, and, drawing to the end of his talk, he sketched a small fiction, an account of a recurring situation in which oppositionists find themselves, a sort of parable of dissent.

...An institution is at work, its members assembled to consider options, arrive at judgements, make decisions. It is probably an academic committee, but it might equally be an editorial conference at the BBC or a debate in parliament. There are proposals, comments, suggestions, counter-proposals. The room is alive with reasonable, constructive discourse. But then another voice is added: perhaps unexpected, perhaps confusing, at all events unwelcome. 'You can't say that', some authority declares. For what has been added is not merely false, perhaps not false at all, but fundamentally out of context, out of register, out of order. It's simple, whichever words are chosen for emphasis: YOU - CAN'T - SAY - THAT. And now, back to business. But no. Even before sensible people have finished nodding their agreement, the awkward voice is raised again: 'But that is what I came here to say'...

I like this story very much. Williams liked it too: he used it more than once. But its full moral force applies more narrowly than it may immediately appear to. Most if not all institutions contain within themselves actual or possible alternatives. These alternatives may be strongly contrasted, and the choices they give rise to may be bitterly fought out. But they are variations within something that does not itself vary. Individuals or groups who stand for such alternatives may be thought old-fashioned or foolhardy or stupid or whatever, but they are not out of order. They are unlikely to be told, 'You can't say that'. Only oppositionists — those whose demands threaten the common sense and basic rules of the institution — are liable to this prohibition.

The distinction between alternatives and oppositions — the terms are Williams's own — is decisive, and it is implicit in his story. But there is a further restriction that I want to mark. The terms of the institutional warning are generic: it could be anyone in authority facing any challenge. But the terms of the response are quite different in kind. There are many ways of expressing defiance, but the particular phrasing of this story seems to me to bear the indelible signature of a personality. 'But that is what I came here to say': no one but Raymond would have put it in quite that way. I take the story as an epitome for two reasons, then: first, as a way of remembering the deep and consistent radicalism — both political and intellectual — of his work. (This cannot be taken for granted in fields of study where even the most complacent are given to the rhetoric of 'subversion'.) Second, to remember the distinctive moral temper of his work, something that is analysable, but which in the end we still call 'personal' and which lent the most generally shared political and cultural positions, in his utterance, an unmistakable signature.

******

The vital impulse of Williams's work was socialism. His political convictions were formed early, in the immediate conditions and influences of home and locality and in the wider crises of the 1930s; politics, in the ordinary, strict meaning of the word, remained a major focus of thought and activity throughout his life. He was a member of the Communist Party for a time and, much later, had a spell in the Labour Party but for most of his life he operated as an

4

independent, active in elections, in campaigns such as Vietnam Solidarity, and in various publishing initiatives. He was a prominent member of the New Left — its outstanding representative, in Edward Thompson's view. He played a central role in the preparation of the *May Day Manifesto*.

Williams was also, from early days, a writer — of plays and stories, later of novels and films. That impulse too was lifelong, and the work that resulted — the Welsh trilogy, *The Volunteers*, *Loyalties*, — is far closer to the centre of his concerns than many readers have understood.

Then, from his later twenties onwards, Williams was a teacher of literature, first in adult education, then at Cambridge. So, his writerly interest in literature and drama was associated with the perhaps more systematic or wide-ranging enquiries of a critic and historian; and his socialist concern with audiences and readerships actual and possible, assumed immediate, practical significance in the circumstances of teaching outside the formal education system. Out of this dialogue of commitments came the theme and the research programme for which above all he became famous: culture and the analysis of culture.

Williams's opening move was to reconstruct the history of thinking about culture in England. This was the work of his best-known book, *Culture and Society*, in which he showed how in the course of the nineteenth century, the term 'culture' had come to mean a body of work — typically, literature, the arts and philosophy — that incarnated values of general and even timeless validity: a 'court of human appeal' set above and often against the ordinary life of societies. Conceived in this way, 'culture' was 'an abstraction and an absolute' remote from historical forces and from the contrasting values that form the ordinary substance of social conflict. It was, correspondingly, an exclusive sphere of existence, drawing upon a tiny range of active contributors and often inaccessible to all but a minority. From these characteristics, 'culture' drew its distant, imperishable authority over society.

Beginning with the critical analysis of *Culture and Society*, then continuing with the series of theoretical and historical studies initiated in *The Long Revolution*, Williams set out to dislodge this tradition, to rethink the whole idea of culture, to fashion appropriate methods for analysing it, to clarify perspectives for socialists working within it. The 'culture' that now emerged was neither 'abstract' nor 'absolute' but fully historical, embodied in the changing life of concrete societies. The human values that it mediated were not of any special, universal character, were not at all privileged, but simply the changing values of whole societies. *Whole* societies, Williams insisted, not exceptional spirits; culture was the process of learning and communication in which all social beings are involved all the time, as a condition of living at all. To analyse a culture was to look at 'a whole way of life'. Now, culture considered in this way is not authoritative in the way that the received humanistic tradition took it to be. But the seeming paradox is that while Williams's analysis divested 'culture' of its presumptive *authority*, he was led, quite logically, to make very strong claims for its general social *efficacy*. Here lies one of his boldest initiatives in the Marxist tradition. If culture — the whole complex work of making sense — is a constitutive aspect of all social activity, then cultural institutions and practices surely play a key role in maintaining existing social relations and, correspondingly, in any struggle to transform them. The idea of cultural *politics* assumes a precise and weighty significance.

Two points must be made about this new programme of cultural analysis. First, it is not simply an extension of the field of interest usually associated with literary studies. If it were only that, it would not be new at all, but merely a left-wing reproduction of the old humanist cultural criticism, which was proudly anti-specialist. Of course, in one immediately visible respect, Williams's work did move outwards from a base in literature, to include the press, advertising, language, television and cinema. But this extension came about as part of a wholesale reconstruction of 'culture' in general. At the same time as trying to develop concepts and methods appropriate to the analysis of particular areas of culture — television, for

6

example — Williams was developing certain key concepts that framed his analysis of *all* culture.

Chief among these is the concept of *convention*. At its most abstract and general, this refers to the psychological proposition that human perception is not naturally determined. There is no natural way of seeing; rather we *learn* how to see, and the patterns of seeing are themselves variable. Then there is the colloquial sense of the word, which is also called upon in Williams's usage. A 'convention' is a social arrangement or understanding, formal or not, conscious or not — a way of relating to (some) others. Finally, there is the meaning most familiar in traditional literary studies, where a convention is a recurring formal device or topic. Say, the habit of starting a story in the middle or of resolving its conflicts through a legacy and a wedding. Now, conventions have led a thankless life in much literary criticism, where certain post-romantic clichés are evergreen. Either they clearly *are* conventions, in which case they are inauthentic and of little meaning; or the text in question is felt to be authentic and meaningful, in which case it can't possibly be the work of mere conventions. The cumulative force of Williams's use of the term is directed against all such commonplaces. All writing, all culture is conventional. The figures and topics of writing are the textual substance of ways of seeing, schemes of perception, and these are at bottom specific social understandings. The concept of convention opens a perspective in which forms *and* contents, texts *and* societies, can be held in relationship, without abstraction or reductionism. It is the analytic key to an understanding of culture as the process whereby historical, social beings make sense of themselves in their world. Not merely a rhetorical concept, not merely a psychological concept, not merely a sociological concept, it is part of a genuinely distinctive development of theory and analysis to which, eventually, Williams gave the name 'cultural materialism'.

My second point is this. It follows from what I have been saying that 'cultural materialism' cannot simply settle into place as one of a range of perspectives in literary and cultural studies. In principle, it seeks to recast such studies altogether. But it cannot, unless in

7

exceptional local conditions, expect such clear victories. This may seem a needless observation, but naive notions of 'progress' are more widespread than you might think in radical literary studies. Raymond Williams was exceptionally strongly committed to rational discourse, to a belief in the efficacy of argument. But he never forgot the non-rational sanctions, the brute power of institutions that is mustered on the other side, for use when the arguments grow too wearisome or disruptive. His work was integrally and avowedly socialist, produced against the conventions of his formal training and his profession, against the conservatism of institutions such as his own. It was from beginning to end a project of *opposition*.

******

Which brings me back to the closing line of the story: 'But that is what I came here to say'.

There are, as I've said already, many ways of giving voice to resistance; the special quality of this one is that, in it, all distinction between thinking and being is left behind. Positions, commitments are formed in a life and are in turn lived, as effort, as a way of being. Specifically, the phrasing summons up the ideal of a biographical journey, a purposeful journey: I have come to this place, from somewhere else, and I have this to say. Williams's personal journey from a working-class home in a small Welsh village to a position of eminence in an extraordinarily privileged university is well known to his readers. We see a very striking version of it in *One Pair of Eyes: Border Country*. And what we see there is not — need it be stressed? — yet another self-engrossed story of the pain of the scholarship boy, nor an exemplary tale of a self-made socialist intellectual, but a reflection, through one life, of the intricate weaving of continuity and change in a general social history. A preoccupation with the interplay of class solidarities and class antagonisms with relationships of kin and settlement — a preoccupation with the changing and changeable meanings of what he called 'community' — was central to Williams's political thinking. It is there most evidently in *Border Country*, but equally in the late interview with Kim Howells (in *Divided Kingdom*), where he probes the real and bogus communities

8

of language, nationality and economic interest summed up in what he called 'the Yookay'. And in all of this there is the voice of someone who, as a matter of pride or at least of self-respect, as a matter of responsibility and in any event as a matter of fact, knows himself a part of this unfinished history.

This strong sense of a thinking, feeling, speaking individual is one shared by very many of Williams's readers. Even the most impersonal of his prose writings bear the mark of a compelling personality. The personal loss that was so widely felt at the time of his death was a direct sequel to the strong feelings of personal respect and affection that he attracted during his life from many thousands of people who had never had direct contact with him. The television programmes to which he contributed are very rich, culturally and politically. But among their special pleasures — which writing can only affect or seem to give — are the images of Raymond himself, the bodily postures, the facial expressions; and the voice, insisting — quietly, but insisting just the same — on what he came here to say.

(This is a transcription of the presentation made under the title 'The Work of Raymond Williams' for the day event 'A Tribute to Raymond Williams' at the NFT, 1 October 1988.)

Give Us This Day

Joy Williams

I chose this film because it is about Robert Noonan, a socialist writer who lived and worked in Hastings from 1901 to 1910. Raymond and I lived there with our children in the 1950s, some of the most important years of his working life.

Noonan wrote *The Ragged Trousered Philanthropists*, under the name of Robert Tressell, about his experiences as a painter and decorator, though he was in fact a signwriter, and of his attempts to put across socialist ideas to his workmates in the town he called Mugsborough. Inevitably, he failed to convince them. Life was too hard for them to even think of change. The insecure and disorganised casual workers were glad to get seven pence an hour, and hoped each year to get through the winter months without being laid off. Noonan himself, often ill and unemployed, finished the novel in 1910, and died soon afterwards. It was not published till four years later, and then in an abridged form.

When we were living in Hastings forty years later, we met many of the same conditions as he had found. There was still high unemployment, and many of the men were glad to go off each week to work in the car factory in Oxford, returning to their families at the weekend. Raymond loved to talk to everyone he met, and spent some time chatting to a Mrs Bowles who, at the age of sixty, and having had eleven children, was still doing part-time cleaning. As an orphan girl she had grown up in one of the now fashionable smugglers' cottages in Rye. Each morning her foster mother baked a basket of fresh bread rolls and wrapped them in a clean white napkin for the child to carry up to the ladies on the hill, so that they could eat them warm for breakfast. Her married life was spent in Hastings where her husband worked as a painter and decorator — like Noonan, for a small wage — though by then it must have been more than the seven pence of earlier days. Each year, just as Christmas was coming up, the men would be laid off. Each year she would look forward to her Co-op dividend to buy some Christmas treats for the children, and each year she had to use it to get the family through till work started again in spring. Like Noonan's workmates, she refused to believe that any action of hers could alter events. She refused to vote in the local elections; 'The forty thieves we call 'em', she said.

The film has some fine shots of Noonan and his friend Bill walking in St Helens Woods on The Ridge above the town, discussing socialism and whether people could ever be persuaded to change their ideas. It is interesting to remember that another young man was also walking in those woods at that time. Teilhard de Chardin, then a novitiate at Ore Place, was picking up fossils and trying to reconcile his received dogma with the concept of evolution. He died in exile unpublished and unrecognised in 1955. *The Phenomenon of Man* was published posthumously. Noonan himself died in a Liverpool workhouse in 1911 on his way to Canada, where he hoped to make a livelihood for himself and his daughter.

The full version of *The Ragged Trousered Philanthropists* had to wait till 1955, when Noonan's biographer Fred Ball brought it out after nine years of effort.

Raymond's admiration of the work was made clear in his Robert Tressell Memorial Lecture, given at Hastings in 1982. This was published with other Robert Tressell lectures by the W.E.A. in 1988, and by Verso in *Writing in Society* under the title 'Ragged-Arsed Philanthropists' which he thought was a more likely title for Tressell to have chosen if convention had allowed it at that time.

The film *Give Us This Day* is a very moving account of Noonan's life and unshaken belief in socialism. I know that Raymond liked it, and hope he would have agreed with my choice.

Three Brothers: Three Generations

John Ellis

Though cinema was an important part of Raymond Williams's work, I found it very difficult to choose a film to represent a substantial part of the aspirations of his project. Clearly, the easy way out would be to choose a title about which he had written in an exemplary way (*Wild Strawberries* or *Days of Hope*). But each case proved inadequate to the breadth and aspiration of his writing. Or perhaps the BBC plays he wrote in the late sixties, where he felt his marginalisation as mere writer once the production was under way, as he observes in *Politics and Letters*. But neither exist any more in the BBC's archives.

It quickly became a search for a thematically and aesthetically apt film. The British cinema, much though I love it, is singularly lacking in appropriate material. Many of its major productions are antithetical; those films which could do justice to Williams's achievement suffer from the problem that he as writer did not encounter: the poverty of resources. A film like Karl Francis's *Above Us the Earth* or even Cinema Action's *So That You Can Live*, though thematically apt, are too much constrained by their budgets to stand, however temporarily, as a fit memorial. Britain, more than any other major European film industry, has suffered from the lack of an 'in-between' cinema, neither routine realism nor aesthetic experimentation, that might provide examples of a wide-ranging critical realism of the type that Williams seemed to desire. For I think such a desire can be discerned behind the rather inadequate debate (in *Screen* and elsewhere) about the concept of 'realism' and his defence of the work of Loach, Garnett, Allen etc. in the seventies. And it can definitely be found in his own fiction output.

Two French films came to mind immediately. Both were directed by Jean Renoir, who nowadays seems to have become an unfashionable figure. He might stand, for a season at least, as a representative of the cultural isolation and neglect that has sometimes also been Williams's lot. But the wonderful elusiveness of Renoir is tricky to fit with the principled basis of Williams's work. The thirties and the French experience of the Popular Front would be the one moment where Renoir's feel for people in agonisingly difficult situations would meet with Williams's political perspective on the personal. This is so simply because Renoir's characters of the mid-thirties are facing all the problems of political change with and within their own cultures. Also, the Renoir of *Toni* is especially alert to questions of regionality within this process. But *La Règle du jeu* from the end of the decade has too much resignation, *La Grande Illusion* is concerned with the experience of war, imprisonment and camaraderie, which were not explicit concerns of Williams (though his role as tank commander is carefully noted in the biographies of old Penguin editions). The films that might fit would be *Le Crime de M. Lange*, with its acute observations of popular cultural forms (the Wild West novels) and its faith in co-operation rather than capitalism. But in the end this wonderful film is motivated more by simple hope than by a political programme produced by a long and painful reflection on the facts of modern existence.

La Marseilleise might well have been my choice. Here is a film concerned with popular attitudes to cataclysmic political change. Its central device is an artistic creation brought from a regional centre to the capital as a vital contribution to the revolution. The different levels of political involvement and sophistication play a large part in the unfolding of the tale. And the film itself, uniquely to my knowledge, is the product of a direct relationship between audience and film production. The finance was raised by subscription, by people paying in advance to see the film, rather than as a speculative venture. This novel form of financing might work only in extraordinary political circumstances: film-making is notoriously too untrustworthy an industry for it to become a routine way of financing, unfortunately. But in the great anniversary year of 1989, I would hope that *La Marseilleise* would be widely circulated again.

Further consideration of French cinema brushed against certain moments of Godard (*Tout va bien* for instance), but Godard is too much of a wilful anti-stylist to be appropriate.

In the end, then, my choice settled on the Italian political situation and the cinema it has produced. The obvious choice was a film by Francesco Rosi. Rosi's work is crossed by many themes consonant with those of Williams, and particularly with Williams's novels. Rosi is rare enough as a socialist director who has continued to be able to produce realist fiction films. But his realism has always strained at the edges, under the pressure of his perceptions of reality. *Hands Over the City* has a wonderful unevenness of effect due to its use of people, particularly politicians, 'playing' themselves. *The Mattei Affair* is particularly disjointed, and has no satisfying end as its central character dies in mysterious circumstances. Rosi's cinema fictions seem to me to be characterised by the same search for an adequate structure that Williams undertook. And Rosi's concern with the divide between the North and South (the country and the city); his refusal to simplify arcane political structures; his immediate sense of the complexities of personal negotiations with political realities: all these are major themes that also run through Williams's work.

My choice of *Three Brothers* is not because it is 'the best' of Rosi's films or 'my favourite' (which might be *Hand Over the City* or, another film possible for this season, *Christ Stopped at Eboli*), but because of its peculiar aptness to Williams's project. *Three Brothers* is hugely ambitious: it is an attempt (and there were others at the time) to analyse 'where Italy is now' in 1979. The moment in question was the Italy after the abduction and execution of Aldo Moro, when urban terrorism had a traumatic grip on the everyday life of Italian city-dwellers: a moment which ten years later already appears historically remote, at least in Italian politics. As a result, Rosi's film appears unexpectedly raw and unpolished, a contrast to some other of his more recent work, or even *Illustrious Corpses*. Its ostensible subject is the visit of three brothers, all living a modern urban existence in the North, to the southern farm where they were brought up, for the funeral of their mother. The mother's death features but marginally; the real subject of the film is the jostling of different approaches to modern Italy, which at that point was dominated by the question of urban terrorism.

Rosi presents terrorism as a problem of political anger: at once a moral and a political question whose solution lies outside the power of any individual within the film. This leads sometimes to a rather programmatic speechifying in one or two scenes. But the characters are not cyphers for a debate. Their problems are not purely political, and their responses are conditioned by their personalities. Then laid across the active adult dilemmas of the three brothers is a sense of generations and history: their aged father in his gleaming white southern farm, and Nicola's young daughter Marta. The lyrical passages of the film chiefly concern Marta and her grandfather, and stretch its perspectives both into the past and into the future. Seen as at a remove from politics because of their ages, they provide the film with an emotional core whose directness counteracts the emotional difficulties of the three brothers.

Each brother stands for a different current in contemporary Italian society: the idealistic Rocco runs a reformatory; Raffaele is a judge, a prime terrorist target; Nicola works for Fiat in Turin and is under threat of dismissal. Each has rapidly sketched personal circumstances which intensify their central dilemmas. Yet the film escapes a programmatic structure to the extent that it allows conventional realism to fray at the edges. Sequences appear that are, loosely, a character's dreams, day-dreams or memories. The opening sequence is Rocco's dream; their father hallucinates (or is it a dream?) a haunting farewell to his wife on the sun-drenched track to their farm. Later, there are other flashbacks and dreams including Rocco's ludicrous, literal image of a 'clean-up' of drugs and crime. All of these fracture the surface of the film, introducing different registers of emotion which qualify and clarify the present. The status of each sequence is relatively clear, even though the conventional introductory devices are understated — making an initial viewing of the film a slightly unsettling experience.

One sequence obstinately refuses to settle into any one of the conventional categories of inserted sequence, however. This is Nicola's scene with his northern wife in Turin. For dream or day-dream, it contains too much self-criticism for the kind of person Nicola is; yet the tentative reconciliation at its conclusion must be a form of fantasy or wish-fulfilment because of the way that his separation from his wife is discussed in the rest of the film. The sequence has no certain status: it could well be understood as a flash-forward to Nicola's return to Turin after time with his daughter and the mourning of his mother.

Uncertainty about the status of this sequence of Nicola spreads to the subsequent vision of judge Raffaele. This begins mundanely enough. He leaves his office and has a charged yet desultory conversation with a colleague about the impossible situation in which they find themselves as a result of threats of assassination if they take on 'terrorist' cases. We then follow a bus within which an assassination suddenly takes place. The victim is revealed eventually as being Raffaele himself. He awakes with a start. The moment is dramatic; there is no bathos; we do not feel that we have been tricked by the film, though this is what, in effect, has happened. Perhaps this does not feel like a trick because it echoes the dynamic of the earlier sequence where the father bids farewell to his wife, which defines itself as imagined only in its second half. In this case, one sequence of uncertain status (Nicola's) has given way almost immediately to another whose status is made clear only in retrospect. The revelation of the judge's dream as dream reorients us definitively. However, in our uncertainty about the status of the sequence as it unfolds, we tend to take it as another probable flash-forward. Our shock at the revelation of the dead Raffaele is very different from that which would accompany a conventional 'dream sequence'. It is used to convey the intensity of Raffaele's everyday fear, one that he cannot confide to anyone around him. The realist organisation of the film reasserts itself.

Yet it is exactly a realism under stress. It can achieve a necessary moment of emotional impact only by breaking itself momentarily but definitively. From this point on, many aspects of the film might well be construed as more subjective than they are. The uncertainty lingers wherever the relative status of a sequence or shot is not heavily stated. Does Rocco imagine getting up in the morning, making coffee all by himself, then gazing from the window and seeing his two brothers weeping, each alone, at different corners of the courtyard? The image is apt enough for these three self-engrossed people, but the shot, with its marked point-of-view set-up (through an upstairs window) could be seen as Rocco's understanding of his two brothers rather than something observed by the narration itself from Rocco's physical point of view. The latter is highly likely, but the instability of the film's realism allows a suspicion of the former. Such an instability is a strength rather than a weakness. It springs from the urgency and complexity of the situation it addresses, rather than any failure of script planning or *mise en scène*.

Three Brothers resolutely refuses to deal only with the immediately contemporary. If anything, the film is critical of the self-engrossment that is forced upon the brothers in their attempts to grapple with contemporary life. This is why it is appropriate as a film to commemorate Raymond Williams's achievement. For his work, fictional and critical, moves between the radically different registers of existence that *Three Brothers* also deploys. At one level there is the essential realisation that, as Nicola says: 'the upheavals in our lifetime are caused by those who've used us as they pleased, hurling us to wherever it suited them best', and he adds, crucially, 'I carry those upheavals around inside me'. But at another level, there is a different register of time: that which made the long revolution into a *long* revolution despite the manifold local cruelties and apparent changes which accompanied it. In the space of a film, these can be communicated only within the relationship between grandfather and granddaughter, with all the risks of romanticisation that this implies. But for Williams, the dual awareness of the immediacy of individual circumstances and the enduring nature of culture could be expressed in a much more complete way, both in criticism and in the novelisation of whole structures of feeling.

Three Brothers is a film which encapsulates many of Williams's characteristic concerns, and in a realist fictional form which I believe to be the filmic equivalent of the methods of his novels.

I Started Out with Renoir But Finished Up with Rachel Roberts

Alan Lovell

The first film course I ever taught was called Realism in the Cinema. It was an attempt to apply to films ideas about the relationship between politics and literature Raymond Williams was developing in the late 1950s.

The heart of the course was an examination of some of Jean Renoir's films: *Le Crime de M. Lange, La Grande Illusion, La Bête humaine, La Règle du jeu.* When I was invited to contribute to this season, my first thought was to choose one of these films.

Memory tells me my efforts to apply Williams's ideas to Renoir's films were clumsy and naive. It doesn't tell me the enterprise was misconceived. If Williams had been concerned with the cinema when he was first thinking about realism, I'm sure he'd have focused on Renoir's work.

Renoir's films, especially those of the late 1930s, fit comfortably into Williams's concept of realism. The drama is created out of the way human impulses towards co-operation and mutual support are frustrated by class barriers. Yet they keep reasserting themselves. The characters in the films have an individual vividness. There's an evident sympathy for ordinary people.

I'm sure Williams would have been curious about Renoir's relationship with the Popular Front. He'd have been intrigued by Renoir's efforts to get films financed by the Unions and socialist groups.

I could have happily settled for *La Grande Illusion* or *La Règle du jeu* as my choice of film. Both of them have a substantial quality which would make them very appropriate salutes to Raymond

Williams. It was only after considerable thought I decided against them.

I had two kinds of reason for thinking a Renoir film wasn't the ideal choice. The first was to do with some important differences between Renoir and Williams.

1. Williams didn't share Renoir's nostalgic attachment to the aristocratic ideal. This isn't just a matter of varying social sympathies. It's a sharp, defining difference. Contrast the presentation of aristocratic, country house life in *La Règle du jeu* with Williams's remarks in *Politics and Letters*: 'I found it necessary to say in the crudest way that these houses were primarily sites of exploitation and robbery and fraud.'

2. Throughout Renoir's work, life in the natural world always inclines towards an idyll. Although Williams was as sensitive to the natural world as Renoir, there's no sense of an idyll attached to it in his work. It's almost always seen in the context of human labour which is laborious, exhausting and exploited.

3. Renoir's art always emphasises performance. It's also marked by a powerful sense of theatricality. Williams is suspicious of performance. His dramatic writings don't have a strong sense of live theatre. In another context, his suspicions of Aneurin Bevan came from a distaste for Bevan's theatricality. In his criticism and his fiction, Williams sets up an untheatrical relationship with his audience/readers. It's a considered, sober relationship he aims for. You can't imagine Williams presenting himself as a performing bear like Renoir does in *La Règle du jeu*!

The second kind of reason for deciding against a Renoir film was my sense that it wouldn't fully represent my own involvement with Williams's work. It would have represented the beginnings only.

From my attempts to relate Williams's ideas to Renoir's films, I took away a substantial interest in the relationship between socialist politics and realist art. What I didn't get any purchase on was modernism. Williams's ideas helped me to 'see' *La Grande Illusion* better. They weren't so helpful for 'seeing' *La Règle du jeu*, even though I preferred it.

I came to modernism by another route: partly through surrealism, especially Luis Buñel, Jean Vigo and Georges Franju's films; partly through Joan Littlewood and Theatre Workshop (which led on to Brecht). It was much later I came to think about Williams and modernism.

In the early 1970s, the dynamic impact of structuralism (shorthand for a mixture of Marxism, semiology and psycho-analysis) on film theory and criticism put modernism firmly on the agenda. I was excited by the intellectual range and boldness of structuralist ideas. I was particularly interested in its re-examination of the relationship between aesthetics and politics.

But from the beginning I was unsympathetic to the politics structuralism generated. Sharing Williams's social origins and being strongly influenced by his arguments about working-class culture, I was very uncomfortable with the description of the working class as 'passive'. It seemed like a replay of old positions.

My political objections led to an increasing distance from structuralism. The account of the working class was central to the relationship it proposed between aesthetics and politics. The position which was developed saw modernism (defined in anti-illusionist terms) as the weapon to combat the realism which was thought to dominate film and television. It was this realism which produced the passivity of the film and television audience.

Modernism and realism were set directly against each other. While I've never been a champion of realism, I respect its achievements (the influence of Williams is obvious). Nor was I an uncritical enthusiast for modernism. I was frequently put off by its elitism and inaccessibility — this feeling was much strengthened by the films which came out of the structuralist climate!

I became increasingly confused: uncertain about my aesthetic commitments; intellectual excitement warring with political hostility; theoretical interests conflicting with populist instincts.

Whenever I was politically confused or intellectually uncertain, my habitual response was to look to Raymond Williams for guidance. How would he respond to the structuralist account of the working class, to the hostility of realism, to the espousal of modernism? I became particularly intrigued about his response when I discovered that a number of the people most actively expounding structuralist positions were pupils of his.

Evidently, Williams had a mixed response to structuralism. He was critical of some of its central positions. But there were aspects he responded positively to — he was strongly attracted by the interest in linguistics.

His most important contribution to the debate was for me his defence of realism and his refusal of the simple-minded opposition, modernism/good, realism/bad. Because of this he was able to avoid the philosophical, political and aesthetic dead ends structuralism ran into (and from which, via post-modernism, it is still trying to extricate itself).

I don't think Williams was able to go far along the road he fought to keep open. He wasn't able to convincingly relate realism to modernism (I'm not persuaded by recent suggestions that he was a crypto-modernist — see *New Left Review*, No. 170).

Williams affirmed his enthusiasms for modernism in a number of places. But lurking around in his consciousness was a Lukacsian distaste for it. In a sense he performed a sleight of hand by transferring this distaste from early modernism onto contemporary modernism:

This is where we need to look at the two faces of 'modernism': at those innovative forms which destabilised the fixed forms of an earlier period of bourgeois society but which were then in their turn stabilised as the most reductive versions of human existence in the whole of human history. The originally precarious and often desperate images — typically of fragmentation, loss of identity, loss of the very grounds of human communication — have been transferred from the dynamic compositions of artists who had been, in majority, literally exiles, having little or no common ground with the society in which they were stranded to become at an effective surface a 'modernist' and 'post-modernist' establishment. This, near the centre of corporate power, takes human inadequacy, self deception, role-playing, the confusion and substitution of individuals in temporary relationship, and even the lying paradox of the communication of the fact of non-communication, as self-evident routine data. (*Towards 2000*, p. 141.)

However, I was emboldened enough by Williams's good sense to think that a political aesthetic might be constructed out of a positive attitude to both realism and modernism. I got a dazzling confrontation of my belief when I came across *The Book of Daniel*. E.L. Doctorow's novel is an exhilarating combination of realist narrative and naturalist description with theoretical digressions, changes of viewpoint, quotations and allusions. It demonstrated conclusively that realism and modernism could be brought into a creative relationship.

Combining political intelligence with aesthetic vitality, Doctorow's novel represents for me the kind of art Williams was working towards. Because of this my choice of film is *Daniel*, the screen version of the novel.

I know it's a second order choice. It's the novel I want to mark — the film's a much more limited work. But because the novel so precisely and imaginatively symbolises for me the effect of Williams's work. Because Williams's interest in film was so strongly mediated by his interest in literature. And because the film is an honourable version of the book (it was scripted by Doctorow), I'm very happy to choose it.

There's another reason why I think *Daniel*'s an appropriate choice. Doctorow's novel is based on the lives of the alleged atomic spies, Julius and Ethel Rosenberg. The film is strongest in its description of one of the shabbiest and most frightening periods of the twentieth century: the late 1940s/early 1950s. The Cold War was intensifying. In Korea it was being transformed into a hot war. Some form of nuclear war seemed a distinct possibility. The combination of Stalinism and McCarthyism was creating a deranged world of spies, atomic secrets, germ warfare, traitors, informers, turncoats and inquisitors.

In this period and through his reaction to it, Raymond Williams crucially developed his intellectual, moral and political identity. Bravely and in relative isolation, he was a conscientious objector to military service in Korea. Distancing himself from Stalinism without, as so many anti-Stalinists did, becoming a supporter of Western capitalism, he created a space to think creatively and begin the intellectual project which was to be so influential and for which so many people are in his debt.

******

Raymond Williams's relationship with Wales was a complicated one. We'll understand his work much better when it's fully taken account of. Sharing a Welsh background with Williams, I wanted to mark the Welsh connection in some way.

If a film had been made of *All Things Betray Thee*, I might have made that my overall choice. Gwyn Thomas's novel is a project rather like Doctorow's: a political subject (it's based on the nineteenth century Merthyr uprisings) treated with a respect for realism and a desire to go beyond it — in this case through using some of the qualities of the ballad.

It's a curious, uncertain, powerful novel which deserves to be better known, as does all of Thomas's fiction. Raymond Williams did his bit for the book by writing an introduction for its recent republication.

In the absence of a screen version of *All Things Betray Thee* (two attempts were made to film it), I've tried to mark Williams's relationship to Wales in a different way.

When I first discovered Williams's work, I hardly noticed his Welshness. It's not very obvious in *Culture and Society* and *The Long Revolution*. It's the novels which most clearly identify him as a Welshman.

I recently re-read *Border Country*, *Second Generation*, *The Fight for Manod*, *The Volunteers* and *Loyalties* with a great deal of pleasure. To my surprise I liked *Second Generation* best of all. A book which I remembered as somewhat dense and ponderous now emerged as rich, subtle and engrossing. It's a key book for understanding his relation to Wales.

Williams's attitude to Wales was powerfully effected by the non-conformist religion which was dominant when he was growing up. He testified how a revulsion against its puritanical attitudes led him to reject his Welshness during his twenties and early thirties.

Second Generation is the book with which he attempts to come to terms with that puritanism. Its central characters, Kate and Peter Owen, wrestle with their puritan heritage. They want to escape from the sexual and emotional stultification it imposes. But they want to hold on to its moral sense. The steady, absorbed exploration of their struggles gives the book a powerful dramatic charge. A distinctive quality of the book is its concern with the female characters. All of them have a strong presence. Kate Owen is one of Williams's most vivid creations. Her actions are in a precise sense a struggle for liberation; emotional, sexual and intellectual. The account of her anticipates the central concerns of the Women's Movement of the 1970s.

The dramatic impact of Kate's story brought to my mind another Welsh woman who struggled with puritanism; the actress, Rachel Roberts. *No Bells on Sunday*, her published journals, provide a harrowing account of her struggles.

Her fight with puritanism contrasts illuminatingly with that of Raymond Williams. He fought, I think, a limited war. By limiting the war he was able to win some victories. Most important he was able to rediscover his Welsh identity; a very fruitful rediscovery for him.

But in other areas, puritanism still constrained him. It limited his fiction, I think. *The Fight for Manod, The Volunteers* and *Loyalties* all have undoubted qualities. In many ways they're more successful and accessible than *Second Generation*. But they lack its emotional richness; its powerful, if muted, sensuality; its sense of personal exploration and moral risk. Having won some freedom from puritanism through writing *Second Generation*, it's as if he didn't want to risk that freedom by continuing the struggle in a head-on way.

27

The risks of fighting continuous, all out war were demonstrated by Rachel Roberts. Sexually anarchic, an exhibitionist and an alcoholic, she was, in the end, totally defeated. Isolated and hardly able to function at any level, she committed suicide.

She even recognised her defeat in the appropriate puritan terms:

I now face utterly the fact that I had and have serious emotional problems gravely accentuated by alcohol and that I could very well lose my sanity. For all of it I am deeply sorry and deeply ashamed and beg your forgiveness Almighty God.

One of the consequences of her defeat was that, unlike Raymond Williams, she wasn't able to rediscover her Welsh identity. Her will stipulated that she didn't want her ashes brought home to Wales.

But maybe Rachel Roberts did win something out of her battle with puritanism. She established her reputation as an actress in two films, *Saturday Night and Sunday Morning* and *This Sporting Life*. Paradoxically, in both of them she portrayed exactly the kind of characters she was reacting against so violently in her own life. Only somebody with a strong inner sense of the forces which shaped such characters could have played them so convincingly.

For me, her strongest performance is as the repressed, life-denying Mrs Hammond in *This Sporting Life*. So I've chosen that film to mark the puritanism which has so powerfully affected Welsh life and whose importance in Raymond Williams's life I've tried to indicate. I also think the authority of Rachel Roberts's performance is a fine salute from one Welsh artist to another.

There's another reason for choosing *This Sporting Life*. The film is, of course, based on David Storey's novel. I've never been able to read Williams's novels without thinking of Storey's and vice versa.

They have so much in common. Both come from the working class. They employ similar fictional materials: working-class life, manual labour, the effects of puritanical attitudes, characters who grow up to be outsiders but can't abandon their backgrounds. Their writing has the same kind of authority. Both have an obvious relation to D.H. Lawrence.

Yet overall their work has a very different feel. I'm sure a sustained comparison would illuminate an important area of British life and literature...

However, I've come a long way from that adult education class about realism in the Cinema. David Storey and *This Sporting Life*, Rachel Roberts, Gwyn Thomas, *No Bells on Sunday*, *All Things Betray Thee*, puritanism, Wales, the Rosenbergs, the Korean War, realism, modernism, structuralism, E.L. Doctorow and *The Book of Daniel*, the French Popular Front, *La Grande Illusion* and *La Règle du jeu*, Jean Renoir — only Raymond Williams could have provoked and encouraged me to think about and try to connect such rich and various topics.

Blue Scar/Valley of Song

Andy Medhurst

There has been no recent British full-length film with as much right to the title 'independent' as Jill Craigie's *Blue Scar*. Jill Craigie and William McQuitty somehow obtained financial backing and made *Blue Scar* without any distribution guarantees, gambling on the Quota Act and the urgent need for British celluloid. Few outside the cinema world will realise the almost suicidal courage required for this act of faith. Circuit booking as first feature, essential to the recovery of outlay, has been refused, although Sir Arthur Jarrett on behalf of British Lion is willing to distribute it. The voice of the trade expert has pronounced that *Blue Scar* possesses no general audience appeal, though three sneak previews at large London suburban cinemas were unanimously favourable. (*News Chronicle*, 11/4/49.)

What is so startling, and so fascinating, about *Blue Scar* seen forty years later, is that it is a British feature film that is consciously political, avowedly socialist. In an early scene Olwen's brother, played by Kenneth Griffiths, is seen reading *Tribune*, but there are no glaring close-ups of this, none of the heavy-handed nudging that one would usually expect. No, his reading of the magazine is unobtrusively integrated into the general picture of the family at home.

It is a film that has its awkward moments, undoubtedly, and these seem to spring from the uneasy fusion of documentary influence with the demands of dramatic narrative. *Blue Scar* is happiest with its scenes of mining, industrial disputes, and the rich, full images of community life, such as when we see the whole village of Abergwynfi streaming up the mountainside to watch the football match. 'There's a spirit in the valleys,' Tom says to Olwen, 'something that keeps us together. You don't find that in the big cities.' The visual expression of that spirit is captured in the film's documentary strand.

It doesn't sentimentalise, though. The streets of Abergwynfi are drab and harsh, with broken pavements and a complete absence of any cinematic beautifying. Olwen wants to escape from this, despite any nourishing 'spirit' it may contain, and the narrative of her journey to Cardiff and London, leaving the valley and the loyal Tom, forms the second, melodramatic strand of the film.

At the university in Cardiff she shares a room with two alarmingly upper-class women, and goes out for dinner with Collins, the English industrial psychologist. The film cuts from this meal to the accident in the mine, from surface luxury to underground suffering — even, perhaps, from superstructure to economic base. The former is built on the latter, it implies crudely but effectively.

Olwen's life in London confirms her loss of 'spirit'. She lives in a tiny flat, surrounded by caricatured members of the literary and artistic set, and when Tom comes to visit she offers him a gin sling. Needless to say, the emotional and political logic of the film propels him back to Abergwynfi and the dependable arms of Glenys.

Blue Scar is not a great film, too many of its scenes are unsure of which way to turn, to documentary or to melodrama, but it is unique in its intentions. What it could have benefited from is the knowledge that melodrama itself is intensely political. There is one hint of this: when Tom goes to the miners' library and reads a volume of socialist literature, we see the page and hear the words, but we also see superimposed images of Olwen and Collins dancing, a whirling waltz that reveals Tom's intense jealousy. This brief overlapping of politics and fantasy has an intensity and complexity that marks it out from the rest of the film.

Whatever *Blue Scar*'s limitations, its achievement can only be magnified by a comparison with *Valley of Song*. Here, only three years later, the same landscapes, even some of the same actors, are pressed into service to perform a slight piece of sub-Ealing comedy, a whisp of Celtic whimsy that delights in all the stereotypes that *Blue Scar* strenuously sought to avoid. In a way reminiscent of Robert

Graves's poem 'Welsh Incidence', *Valley of Song* offers a Wales composed of nothing but gossips and chapel. Its workers are primarily shopkeepers and small business people, so the issues of nationalisation and socialism so central to Craigie's film are bypassed entirely. The sheer comic verve of the acting, particularly from Rachel Roberts as Bessie the Milk, makes the film hard to dislike, but after *Blue Scar* it can only be seen as a retreat into cosiness.

Ms Rhymney Valley, 1985

Dai Smith

The miners' strike is being represented as the last kick of an old order. Properly understood, it is one of the first steps towards a new order. This is especially the case in the emphasis they have put on protecting their *communities*... What the miners, like most of us, mean by their communities is the places where they have lived and want to go on living, where generations not only of economic but of social effort and human care have been invested,and which new generations will inherit. Without that kind of strong whole attachment, there can be no meaningful community. (Raymond Williams, 1985.)

Most of the things, and moods, that made the 1960s invigorating and fashionable by-passed South Wales. New directions were limited to re-housing people in tower blocks plonked with mindless aplomb on empty plateaux or naming sprawling council estates after Welsh castles or Harold Wilson. Older struggles seemed more real and more dispiriting as a Labour government hastened to run down the coal industry and local Labour administrations thought only of maintaining the *status quo*. The reversal of expectation in the 1970s was as abrupt as it was exciting. Suddenly, it seemed that the well-springs of deeper energies in the coalfield were being tapped again. South Wales, in the strikes of 1972 and 1974, was at the forefront of a regional and occupational revolt that was unshackled from the chains of false loyalties. The talk amongst younger people was of '1926' and of 'Revenge for what they did to us then'. The caution beaten into the bones through the intervening decades was exorcised by a heady mix of underground folklore and startling victories. Perhaps something of the febrile spirit of the Sixties had, after all, penetrated the carapace of survivalism that the valleys had cultivated against the danger of all enthusiasm.

Certainly it was that quality which now created fresh, yet echoing, initiatives in South Wales — in the arts, in historiography, in adult education. And it was because of a determination to connect such matters so that they might not, once more, go underground to fester into mere myth that Raymond Williams was invited to speak at the Polytechnic of Wales in 1976. The occasion was a weekend conference, organised by the Welsh Labour History Society and the South Wales N.U.M., around the issues and the history of the General Strike and Miners' lockout of 1926. These were twinned since, for areas like South Wales, they were never separate in experience. On a Saturday morning in May, half a century after that industrial rebellion that was also a social phenomenon, Raymond stood up in front of an audience of 400 people. His listeners varied widely the one from the other, in age, sex, occupation and education. Many had never even heard of his name. Most had not read any of his work. His was not the easiest of tasks that morning. It was not lectures to which they were accustomed but the drill of rhetoric and the clarity of orders.

They were given neither. Instead, he spoke for an hour in a conversational, yet audible, tone that eschewed all platform trickery in favour of a dialogue. This was conducted with himself but always in such a way as to engage his vast, disparate audience in his own passionate seriousness. His notes consisted of a few scribbled lines on a postcard yet he never faltered since he never strained for effect. This was a man thinking with us, making us think, offering us his thought, never deigning to think for us: if this was culture then, the audience sensed, culture was ordinary. What underlined how remarkable a performance he gave — as an intimate communication with others it was an experience the printed talk cannot, fine as it is, quite convey — was the challenging content of the lecture. In Pontypridd, in the centre of the coalfield, amidst the buzzing euphoria of a battle-hardened N.U.M., he spoke, after due acknowledgement of 'the central action', of 'a need to consider the complex social action...in a more mixed situation' and 'the diffused scenes in which the effective struggle for a new consciousness also occurs'.

As we applauded we did not, perhaps, consider how 'the central action', would be fought again but, disconcertingly and confusingly even in South Wales, as a more 'complex social action...in a more mixed situation' in 1984-85. Raymond intervened then, of course, in the direct fashion of supporting the strike with words and deeds. He spelled out how the deep solidarity of South Wales was rooted in a sense, experienced *and* theorised by the people themselves, of what 'culture' and 'community' meant. *He* never apologised for using *these* keywords and it was clear that, in 1984, he took a grim satisfaction in knowing how vital their actual manifestation really was to the class struggle underway. The novels had always striven to explore such intricate connections in the face of obtuse sophistication. Now for *Loyalties* (1985), he broke away from his work-in-progress to etch the lines of continuity and of fracture, and even of betrayal, with acid intent. The novel is a kick against de-humanising reductionism in emotional attachments *and* in political relationships. I believe it is a pre-emptive strike against those who would wish to read off from the downfall of the miners' union and the effective defeat of their action the lesson that their kind of communities and the nature of their political consciousness is outmoded. It is a canard, from right and left, which he detested.

The alternative, as he had pointed out in 1976, was not a frenzied 'recapitulation' of the past nor a managerial 'solution' of the present mess but a freshly imagined sense of our own history as a conscious guide to a self-controlling future. He knew the obstacles. He admitted the difficulties. He did not disguise the defeats. Yet he never ceased to claim that the future *could* be articulated and that history *could* be re-presented. In 1976 he had caused us to be conscious of those necessities and if we cannot replace his exemplary articulation of both the hope and the loss then we can, at least, aspire to his constant recognition that the poetry and the culture and the politics reside in those with whom he classed himself — the ordinary. It is these people, and their inheritance, that we recognise and acknowledge as also extraordinary in the best film to emerge from that 1984-85 conflict. It also happens to be from South Wales.

Early in 1985 I rang Karl Francis, whom I'd met intermittently since 1972, to ask if I could come to watch him shoot some of his new movie. I had heard that it was taking the strike as its subject and I was curious to see how he would make anything so contemporaneous with the events being depicted. Karl readily agreed and later talked to me about his intentions and his ambitions for the film. The piece I wrote appeared, in a much shortened version, when it was screened. In the aftermath of defeat the film attracted scant sympathy and has not been shown since. Now that 1984-85, too, has 'passed into history', I think Karl Francis's wonderful blending of a past conjured up by its symbols with a diurnal grind enlivened by wry self-consciousness and by the provoking, dramatic crisis of the strike itself in the lives of his protagonists is still more impressive. Its combination of bold experimentalism (with facts as well as with film) and underplayed documentary realism (which alludes to the fiction of our factual selves) are features of which Raymond would have approved, and for which he would have saved up some acute criticism. My own appears below in its original form and with the tempered hope which I felt on seeing it in faraway 1985.

******

The Ruperra Social Club is in the mining village of Trethomas which merges with its larger neighbour, Bedwas, towards the bottom end of the Rhymney Valley. On Friday 15 February its main room — dance floor, stage and bar — was alive with people, lights and music. A film crew scurried around the scattered tables and chairs. The leader of the Labour Party was expected at any moment. Neil Kinnock was well known here for the locality had been part of his old Bedwellty constituency. He arrived to considerable applause at the end of a week in which he had told the Prime Minister, in the House of Commons, he could not *quite* bring himself to believe her. When he asked this audience, whose contact he put on like an old, familiar coat, whether he should apologise the crescendo of support was instant. When he suggested Mrs Thatcher should apologise to striking miners for calling them 'the enemy within' the applause was led and sustained from the floor by Terry Thomas, Vice-President of the South Wales miners and by Kim Howells, their spokesman and research officer through the dispute. On the stage Neil Kinnock presented a cheque to the Rhymney Valley Miners' Support groups in aid of the families who had members in jail because of the strike. The cameras stopped and Karl Francis had completed the shooting of his BBC 2 film — *Ms Rhymney Valley, 1985*.

This last sequence encapsulated his determination to marry the 'public' and the 'private'. Since Karl Francis had taken up his commission in the late winter of 1984 he was determined to make a film that would work against those images of the strike to which we became wearily accustomed over its twelve months. He was concerned to show lives which were, at one and the same time, buffeted by daily events and conscious of a need to shape their own framework. Neither the trivial nor the momentous could be separated. Francis had been concerned with these things before and, in *Above Us the Earth* and *Rough Justice*, he had developed his ideas about drama-documentary to show the spiralling effects of pit closures and political strife by concentrating on the individuals who actually experienced the process. Now, this profound dispute brought him back again to his own home village of Bedwas to see if his technique of direct filming of real people (placed but not directed), of real conversation (discussed but not scripted) and of actual events (whose outcome remained unknown in the filming) would produce a film that might explain why South Wales maintained its exceptional solidarity for so long.

Karl Francis has succeeded brilliantly. His film convinces as much by the 'sincerity' of its overall design on our intelligence — it is not a literal film about a documented South Wales served up in pseudo-objectivity on an analytical platter — as by the 'authenticity' of the people and opinions it unswervingly captures. Ordinary people are shown, by their own deeds and words, to be extraordinary. 'Public' figures are focused through the 'private' end of the telescope. Miners comment on the commentary politicians and television offer them about themselves. The integration of the N.U.M., at area and lodge level, with the immediate needs and the wider perspectives of coalfield society is not paraphrased but shown. The picket line at the Abercwmboi Phurnacite Plant, which the one strike-breaker in the Cynon Valley entered, is not seen from a detached distance. We move into the picket line by being on the picket's side — not 'outside looking in', as Francis put it, but 'inside looking out'.

And what we see and hear is not only emotionally disturbing. It is, too, a considered reflection on what made the energy and the suffering possible. The humanity of the world he restores to our sight is conveyed, above all, by humour — a humour that is wry, sardonic and tinged with blackness but also raucous and defiantly joyous. This is a film that does not deny laughter to its serious purpose. The very title is a joke which wraps the package up — the beauty contest for the fund-raising social evening in the Ruperra which will not, despite the ardent hopes of the local Labour Party Chairman, be about 'tits and bums — and what's wrong with a nice body?' but which woman has done most for the strike. In the end there is no separation in competition to be made. We are engaged, early on, by the people whose lives came together in this and other, more desperate, public occasions. The film, cut with stunning precision by Chris Lawrence, gambles everything on the unfolding of its public history being accessible by the act of risking a slow accumulation of detail — women bandying clichés to which the force of the strike restores meaning; an old-timer who 'fought the scabs' in the 1930s fails to light a fire with 'English coal' and reflects that 'It's a sin to get old...you can't keep the idle rich'; a woman watches Neil Kinnock interviewed on TV and irons a silk banner on which is painted the face of Will Paynter, the exceptional miners' leader who died in the last month of 1984.

The woman, Betty, begins the film by walking into view on a housing estate whose appalling disrepair and dereliction is a hollow echo of its proud name, the Lansbury Park Estate. She is our first, unobtrusive guide to the people whose stories in the strike we will follow. Most noticeable of all will be a young, unemployed woman called Charmaine Nind. She is an ex-management trainee sacked for refusing to dismiss a workmate who 'blew up' a computer by accidentally tipping a cup of coffee over it. Since then, eleven 'O' levels and dazzling confidence notwithstanding, she remains victimised — 'Well, when you ring up and say your name is Charmaine Nind, well, it's not like saying Ann Jones, is it?' — and a 1980s representative of her militant grandfather, the legendary Billy Nind, who was himself victimised for eight years for helping drive the scab union out of Bedwas Colliery in the 1930s. Charmaine joins with other women to derive broader political perspective from their instinctive support of the strike. Memories are not burdens to be lugged around mindlessly. They are a shared history which liberate the spirits of people once again engaged in real struggle. Karl Francis mixes with his naturalistic footage some lyrical evocations of people and landscape to combine the future vision and the compromised present. This has always been the vital junction box of South Welsh history and it has never been better represented than by the endless variety of unifying factors released by the strike.

Karl Francis's monumental achievement is that he has discovered a way of depicting this historical process in action. The close-ups of his main protagonists — around the Bedwas Colliery, in the N.U.M. offices, in the running story of preparations for the social evening, over the involvement of women on the picket lines — is counter-pointed by a vibrato intonation that brings the whole landscape and history of South Wales into play. The lodge banners become icons of pride and defiance which the representatives of the Church, winning fresh respect in this struggle, bless. The Moderator of the United Reform Church in Wales tells us 'Jesus was the son of a builder...executed for political as much as religious reasons.' His defeat, too, was not final. Despair and misery co-exist with a gutsy desire to enjoy what can be enjoyed. The 'beauty contest' without competitors proceeds. People jive to a rock 'n' roll beat. Kinnock speaks and, Betty, baby-sitting on the council estate where people strive, against all odds, to make a community, tells a new-born baby that she, a miner's daughter, must be proud. It is she who will *really* be 'Ms Rhymney, 1985'.

'How Welsh Are My Eyes?':
So That You Can Live

Textual Analysis and Political Cinema in the 80s
Noel King

I think the two things that have to be said are: one, that the radical left in Britain has never been more vital or more theoretically informed or more capable of doing all kinds of cultural work; and two, I also think there's never been a greater distance between it and where most of the people who are the objects of its concern, and subjects of its concern, are living and thinking. The distance is very great. (Raymond Williams.)[1]

Today, as we live many...moments of danger as whole histories of struggle are eradicated or threatened with devaluation...we must value above all other signifying practices that cinema (and television...) which made memory fertile, a cinema that can make loss productive, that can turn understanding into resistance and resistance into understanding, a cinema that can help us overcome loss by means of understanding, so that we all can live. (Paul Willemen.)[2]

... So that You Can Live (STYCL) is a film which wants to hang onto notions such as 'individual', 'class', 'lived experience', 'history', all terms which have been submitted to rigorous review over the last few years. Given that the film reactivates this series of contested, problematised categories by bringing some of Raymond Williams's work to bear on the events it depicts, a quotation from Williams should prove a convenient way of starting to discuss the film's considerable achievements:

The simplest descriptive (film) about working-class life is already, by being (filmed) a significant and positive intervention.[3]

What would worry some people about a statement such as that is the way it seems to ignore questions of representation and narrative: a class is thought to exist as an unproblematic, homogenous whole and to have direct access to a class-specific mode of talking about itself. However, *STYCL* is anything but a 'simple descriptive film about working-class life'. It is a film about what it means *now* to live in South Wales, a documentary which was made over a period of five years. Interestingly this five year period means that filming would have started around the time a certain prominence was being given to those documentary films which effected a combination of a form of feminism with labour history/oral history. This form of feminism was, for the most part, essentialist, committed to consciousness-raising (e.g. *Union Maids, With Babies and Banners, The Wilmar 8*, although the more recent *Rosie the Rivetter* and *A Wive's Tale* indicate its continued viability as a film mode) and *STYCL* is a film which carefully detaches itself from this mode, establishes a critical distance from it by placing its major stress on a complicated process of *learning* rather than on more celebratory, triumphalist notions. For example, there is no summoning of archival footage to support the memory of a particular witness-narrator at a particular time; there is no historical overview provided by a voice-over narrator of the kind to be found in those other documentaries which address the women-union relation. Instead, we have Diane, the daughter of the Butts family, sometimes narrating the history of the family over the five year period of Cinema Action's filming and sometimes reading sections of Williams's work.

A different indication of the film's distance from those North American models could be found in the scene towards the end of the film which shows Shirley, at work again, on a picket-line but on its margins, displaced by the male regional organisers and district committee members. If we set this image against the fact that the working population in Wales (usually portrayed by way of stereotypes of miners or steelworkers) has shifted dramatically in recent years to the point where there are now more women employed in industry than men, an interesting reading becomes available. Shirley can then be said to represent, to some extent, the contradictions within Welsh labourism: she is displaying her commitment to a union whose structure remains that of twenty or more years ago, still very much geared towards the traditional male-worker image both in its organisational hierarchy and its rhetoric: her 'place' or 'position' is a reproach to a union which seems unable to adapt itself to the changes it must effect if it is to connect with the fact that women now constitute the main workforce in Wales.

I want now to set out, quite schematically, some areas of criticism of the film which can function simultaneously as ways of entry into it, potential reservations which also constitute specific points of engagement with the film and its politics. These are not criticisms I have invented: they are already circulating, written or said, around the film. The first area relates to disputes over the use of Raymond Williams's work and how it operates in the film. In their review of the film Sue Aspinall and Mandy Merck say

> the use of Raymond Williams's texts (spoken and as inter-titles) are particularly problematic. They are spaced throughout the film, as if to situate the other material within the framework of wider determinations. However, in the absence of other extended extrapolations on this material, the effect of these remarks about complexity and capitalism is often a sense of awe at mysterious forces at work, rather than a sharpening of understanding.[4]

Derrick Price, on the other hand, argued that the extracts from Williams's work used in the film

> serve to link personal familial and community experience to the structure of wider arguments but they are not inserted as external theoretical pronouncements. They advance arguments, make connections and give us access to another discourse through which the events of the film can be examined...
>
> STYCL uses Williams's work to emphasise the connections between past and present; between power, landscape, memory and political action.[5]

The use of Raymond Williams's texts functions in at least two ways. They are there, *recruited to* the film, inserted into the specific context of this particular documentary subject around a Welsh working-class woman unionist and her family and, in one kind of reading, that would be the limit of their utility. It is not a condition of reading these sounds and images to recognise the references to Raymond Williams's writing: there is no necessity to pick up this set of allusions. At another level, however, they address a viewer either assumed to be familiar with the range and importance of Williams's work or else they *constitute* a viewer who will read that work and then work on its relation to the film through a series of further viewings. In this respect the quotations from Williams would be roughly equivalent to, say, the quotations from Mao and Lenin in *Vent d'est*. 'Roughly' because the citing of the work of the son of a Welsh railway employee will have quite specific resonances in a film about a Welsh working-class family and its struggles. While on the subject of the railway, we could consider the shot of a disused railway line, an image would could seem 'quaint' or 'idyllic' to a non-Welsh eye but which speaks quite crucially of de-industrialisation and the consequent problems of public transport for the inhabitants of Wales. Welsh agricultural workers were transformed very rapidly into industrial workers and now, after two or three generations, find themselves cast aside, thrown back onto the land but no longer readily possessing the skills to become agricultural workers. The result is living in isolation, finding it harder to get industrial work and having to travel further and further to get it. Increasingly, *STYCL* shows, the only means of travel has become the company bus which now takes ninety minutes to make a twenty minute journey. We are shown the motorway (to London) which carried traffic *through* Wales but which is quite useless for people *in* Wales — unless they happen to want to go to Bristol or London.

To gloss an image from the film in this way is to open up questions of the status of *regional* film-making, the limits this might set on readings. It allows the film to exert a degree of determinacy over its otherwise unpredictable sites of consumption. Here we might recall Umberto Eco's discussion of Antonioni's documentary on *China* and the fact that some images which, for Western spectators, acquired a positive meaning, had a negative meaning for Chinese spectators:

> The most typical example is the question of the Nanking Bridge which, according to the Chinese newspapers, was presented by Antonioni as if it were on the verge of collapse. Now if you look at the sequence of the Nanking Bridge you will see that Antonioni shoots it in a long travelling shot from a boat which is passing under the bridge. He is shooting it in an oblique way, transversally — in the same way a normal Western movie would shoot a skyscraper or monument: from beneath to try to give the impression of tension and of a leap towards the sky. But this is a stylistic device typical of the Western movie...and I tried to recall how the Chinese today represent, in their propaganda posters, buildings and various other things. They are very frontal, very symmetrical. Therefore, for them, Antonioni's method of shooting expressed trembling, expressed collapse, expressed an unstable situation or, at least, it was possible to take it in this way.[6]

Eco's anecdote provides succinct evidence of the extent to which ways of seeing/reading are historically and culturally situated. Ways of reading are embedded in specific and variable cultural-historical conditions and are not the consequence of some unchanging transcultural, transhistorical human faculty. Our ways of reading do not emerge from within our natures but rather are the consequence of our practical familiarity with specific techniques and conventions in which we are trained and which we (consciously or unconsciously) reactivate.

The image of the disused railways in *STYCL* also opens onto the larger question of the status of *landscape* in the film. For example, Sue Aspinall and Mandy Merck argue that the film

> frequently deploys landscape to produce a sense of melancholy and loss, creating an elegiac mood...the film's sense of loss, of landscapes and communities evacuated by capitalism, proposes the past as its major source of value, the embodiment of a greater sense of community and class identity.[7]

The depiction of landscape in the film is, allegedly, either 'pastoral' or else a 'tourist' version of Wales (beautiful landscapes, historic sites). It seems to me that the landscapes work precisely against this notion/image of Wales, comprising much more a case of 'landscape as industrial archaeology', presenting the traces of the development of an economic process (the exploitation of Wales) and simultaneously posing the textual problem of how to read it (cf the 'ambiguous' image of the railway line). At another stage in the film we see scenes of the family doing some gardening. The background is composed of green trees which might be read as 'picturesque' were they not a 'reforestation' area; that is to say taken *away from* agriculture and used for investments by the city (London), land being used for giant profits as wood becomes an expensive commodity in Europe. The Conservative Party used local Welsh labour and resources to destroy this agricultural land and to plant it full of trees, a redeployment which of course is of no use whatsoever to the Welsh. The National Trust (a public body) supposedly owns the area but the Conservative Government is selling it off piecemeal for long-term investments and it constitutes one of the most lucrative investment areas in the UK finance market.

Still other aspects of 'the land' need to be read. The hills, after all, are quite literally 'man-made' as slag heaps are grassed over or as hills are hollowed out. The hills carry the traces of previous exploitation, the profits of which are nowhere to be found in Wales.

The articulation of images of the landscape with particular pieces of music has provoked the charge of the film's having an overly elegiac tone. 'Elegiac' seems a fair enough description of the main musical motif but it does not follow that one should automatically reject this aspect of the film. If, objectively, the history of the Welsh working class is one of marginalisation and defeat then it is significant to note that *STYCL* neither endorses this state of affairs nor tries to sweep it under the carpet. (Some idea of the situation in Wales in this respect — that is, a divided, subdued working class — can be gained from knowing that some months ago Welsh pits due for closure failed to galvanise the miners into a strike.)

Remarks on the use of music in *STYCL* hinge on whether it is said to be 'too insistent', 'too elegiac', thereby rendering the film defeatist or fatalist-romantic. But the interplay between the musical motif, the

48

music-class scenes and the drummer boys constitutes a pattern in its own right. The class scenes and the drummer boys stand under the sign of 'training/learning' and a notion of the social aspect of music in South Wales. Here, rather than criticising the music presented, it would seem more pertinent to notice the striking *absence* of Welsh choirs. Given that Welsh choirs are the dominant media representation of 'Welsh community' this quite calculated absence should register with the viewer. In addition the drummer boys signify a possible call to arms but in a setting (an abandoned quarry) which says a great deal about the context in which that struggle will take place: a Wales devastated by industrial debris, economic decisions which have (in Williams's telling phrase) been 'taken elsewhere' and which have left nothing but the traces of an industrial history engraved in the landscape.

The aptness of the term 'elegiac' is given further evidence by Raymond Williams's remarks in the *Screen* interview where he speaks of

> the repeated failure, under extraordinary provocation, to generate sufficient collective action...
>
> The problem of action is now within a changed set of social relations, in which the obvious lines of action are not to be simply recovered from some past repertory where people know what the forms of action are (i.e., films such as *Union Maids* would not be the appropriate model for this particular context)...
>
> One wouldn't have projected a Britain with three million unemployed and everything else that's happening, in which there would be so little really effective, sustained levels of action. It's been dispersed, it's been blocked and it's very urgent really to know why. I don't think the film can tell us why but it's one of several explorations of why.[8]

Williams is suggesting that *STYCL* provides an *analytic representation* of the current situation in South Wales, setting out the position from which struggle would begin. While it is true to say that the film does not provide a programme for that struggle this is not so surprising given that it is only quite recently that 'Wales' has begun to be analysed on the left as a specific social formation (c.f. Gwynn Williams writing in *Marxism Today*). But to acknowledge this 'absence' is not, therefore, to say that the film is fatalistic or pessimistic. Far from it. Quite apart from the emphasis on a complicated notion of learning (mentioned earlier) there is, towards the end of the film, the image of the tree held for quite a long time and this, together with an earlier 'winter-treescape', seems straightforwardly to signify 'resistance' and/or 'will to survive'. And, after all, the Butts family *does* survive and continues to fight one way or another.

What are some of the other positive features of *STYCL*? First, it would seem to explode a dominant notion of 'Britishness' (mobilised so comprehensively by Thatcher during the Falklands war) and to oppose what Tom Nairn has dubbed 'the English ideology' by counterposing the historical-social specificity of one of the internal colonies (and Wales was the first of the English colonies).

Second, the film indicates a means of inscribing a number of 'different' rather than simply 'contradictory' discourses without resorting to the strategies of those films which organise their arguments and analyses into a series of sequences/segments. *STYCL* uses more 'simultaneity' of inscription (e.g., the triad: people/landscape/music) without collapsing everything back into a homogeneity of realism. Rather, we have to learn to read different parts of the image as well as different bands of expression: to the extent that this occurs, *STYCL* might be seen to be a film which initiates a long-overdue reinterrogation, retheorisation of *mise-en-scène*. (This seems to be one of the things Godard is doing in *Sauve qui peut* and *Passion*.)

Third, *STYCL* re-opens possibilities for narration and representation without falling into the *puritanical* didacticism (as opposed to 'didacticism') found in some of Godard-Gorin's work. To this extent the film is an example of the shift towards that new form of cinema outlined by Paul Willemen in the quotation cited earlier. *STYCL* manages to present, very accurately, a complex situation, offering a number of possible points of critical engagement for further analysis. It doesn't set out an analysis to be taken or left (though this is not at all a criticism of those which *do* use that strategy).

I have said on a number of occasions that the film is, at one level, a complicated exploration of the conditions under which knowledge and learning take place. Derrick Price noted that 'throughout the film different versions of knowledge, education and history are interrogated for their use-value to the people of South Wales.'[9] And Raymond Williams spoke of

> the emphasis in the film, first, on a woman growing into either available work or into the difficulty of getting any kind of work at all, the role of education, this whole relation between work and learning.[10]

And this theme is then caught up with Diane's reading of Williams's texts. Derrick Price again: 'Read by Diane they are removed from the world of academe, inflected with the accents of ordinary speech and put to work in the service of the people for whom they are written.'[11] Or as Claire Johnston put it: 'The rhythm and grain of the voice transform and reactivate the texts, reappropriating them for the people for whom they were written.'[12]

It is interesting to set these two assessments (concerning the redeployment of Williams's texts) alongside Terry Eagleton's recent work on the history of the institution of criticism in Britain from the Enlightenment through to Raymond Williams, using Habermas's concept of 'the public sphere'.[13] In brief, Eagleton's argument is that criticism initially was political enterprise, a form of cultural politics (around the periodicals, salons and discourse of the eighteenth century) but gradually became academicised via the shrinking of the public sphere, to the point where now in Britain a few hundred people busily review one another's books. If criticism is to regain its role as an important part of determining social strategy then it will involve the construction of a *counter* public sphere. Eagleton cites the work of Raymond Williams as being exemplary in not having respected the divisions between discourses, in always being directed towards oppositional institutions of one kind or another. Owing to the unpropitious conditions in which most of Williams's writing has been done it is writing addressed, as it were, to a *missing* public sphere, to the *possibility* of a counter public-sphere which was not then on the agenda (and still isn't). Consequently, Williams's work was forced back into the academy (as Eagleton's has been) and inevitably shows the marks of that (c.f. in this respect Williams's frequent references to the *blockage* of forces and energies). A film like *STYCL* — by recirculating, recycling Williams's texts — might, in a way, be taking them towards one part of that missing public sphere. Another way of phrasing this would be to say that the film is redistributing Williams's texts in much the same way as Williams has spoken of the necessity for working-class writing to be recirculated. It is not sufficient to stop at the act of recovery or retrieval, the establishment of another area of literary criticism: the texts must be reinserted in new reading formations and this is what the film is trying to do with Williams's own writing.

Much of the film explores notions of families, communities, class and history, all areas on which Williams has written extensively in his own long and often solitary process of learning. The point in the film where the camera tracks along a bookcase in a Workers' Institute Library and cuts (while maintaining the continuity, fluidity of the pan) to working-class inner urban houses, is a point in question. 'We begin to think and feel where we live', Williams once wrote and this refers to books as much as houses, each the product of a particular kind of labour, each a part of the main institutions which sustain a life (c.f. family/union connection).

The film begins with Diane in London, on the balcony of a tall apartment building, explaining that she came to London to see what jobs were available 'because there were none down Wales'. She then has to study again to get a job because education in Wales is 'less' than in England. A bit later the film shifts to an old man sitting in a green valley wondering what it was like one hundred years ago, 'the things that went on then are unbelievable today... Had I known then that, at my age, I would be as interested as this I'd have known a lot more because I'd have asked questions'. Later in the film, during scenes of the GEC strike, the women strikers describe their boss: 'he's such a cunning man, I don't know what school he went to...' and then add, concerning the issues of the strike, their working conditions and wages, 'we can see it now but we couldn't at the time'. These are three very different examples of the relations of learning/education and work, the *work* of learning which might help people to resist that 'world of arrangements beyond us, placed, brought about without people being told'.

As Jane Clarke succinctly described it, *STYCL*

took five years to make. What started as fairly immediate footage of an equal pay strike at a Welsh GEC works in 1976 has over the years had layer upon layer added to become an archaeology of the social, political, cultural and economic forces which shape the lives of a working-class family in South Wales today.[14]

It is a film which speaks to so many areas of current debate: first to questions of working-class cultures and its erosion, showing that certain conceptions of a working-class culture increasingly seem no more than a labourist myth; bingo and billiards have replaced an earlier allegedly more militant culture. A grandmother laments the passing of a time in which songs and stories defined the familial exchanges, replaced now by television and clubs. This is, however, a feature of the film which needs more argument and the point might be to concentrate attention on these popular cultural forms *now* being engaged in by the Welsh working class.

Second, *STYCL* connects crucially with debates concerning conceptions of a 'national cinema': it restates the film-nationalism relation by showing how the specific signifying practice of cinema can intervene in another set of institutions and representations (the writing of history books, in the example of the Workers' Institute Libraries; unionism; the educational system). Here it might be useful to set the film against *The Cheviot, the Stag and the Black, Black Oil*. Despite their obvious differences in modes of circulation (*The Cheviot* being a TV adaptation of a text which already had a certain status and political visibility, *Play for Today* being a mode of exhibition quite different from the kind of circulation/exhibition of Cinema Action's films) each text explores the way a national culture (Welsh, Scottish) has been systematically attacked, suppressed, eroded. Each is concerned with the issue of popular memory as it relates to the possible disappearance for working-class militance, each to some extent mobilises the figure of 'the people/the land/the language' and each is intrinsically implicated in Raymond Williams's writing (McGrath repeatedly speaks of his debt to Williams's work).

It might then be appropriate to use another quotation from Williams as a means of finishing these remarks on the importance of *STYCL* and also as a means of indicating why we should continue to work on/with films of its kind:

> Because we are here. Because the Depression, suddenly, is not a historical period, for the recovery of documents and memories. Because it has come back, is again being imposed on us and we thought that would never happen. Not a literary or historical experience. Unemployment closures; political defeats and divisions; advice to emigrate, anger.[15]

Anger yes. And analysis, oppositional readings which will need to be produced from sites other than that provided by a Steenbeck editing machine.

(This is the second part of a longer article, reprinted from *Undercut* magazine, nos.10/11.)

NOTES

1. 'This Sadder Recognition', Sue Aspinall interview with Raymond Williams, *Screen (incorporating Screen Education)* 23, 3/4 (1982) p.151.
2. Paul Willemen, 'Postscript', *Framework* 18 (1982) p.23.
3. Raymond Williams, 'Working-class, proletarian, socialist: problems in some Welsh novels', in H. Gustav Klaus (ed.) *The Socialist Novel in Britain* (Sussex: Harvester Press, 1982), p.111.
4. Sue Aspinall and Mandy Merck, " 'So That You Can Live', II", *Screen* 23, 3/4 (1982) p.158.
5. Derrick Price, " 'So That You Can Live'; A Welsh Response", *Framework* 19 (1982) p.15.
6.

'Semiotics and Film: An interview with Umberto Eco' by William Luhr, *Wide-Angle* 1, 4 (1977) p.71.

7. Aspinall and Merck, *art cit.,* p.159.
8. Williams, 'This Sadder Recognition', p.147, 150.
9. Price, *art cit.,* p.15.
10. Williams, 'This Sadder Recognition', p.147.
11. Price, p.15.
12. Claire Johnston, 'So That You Can Live: Popular Memory', *Framework* 19 (1982), p.12.
13. See the 'Interview' with Terry Eagleton in *Southern Review* (Adelaide), 17, 1 (March 1983).
14. Jane Clarke, " 'So That You Can Live' I", *Screen* 23, 3/4 (1982), p.153.
15. Williams in Klaus (ed.), p.112.

Fame Is the Spur

Raphael Samuel

Fame Is the Spur (Boulting Brothers, 1947), is a Labour morality, a variant (or inversion) of the age-old fable and tale-type in which a poor boy makes good. Here, it is the boy from the back streets who, fired by the social gospel, is translated from the grime of Manchester to the aristocratic glitter of St James's. He begins his life in the slums, rousing himself, in the film's opening sequence, to the early morning tap of the knocker-up; he ends it, ermined in the House of Lords, and an honoured guest at Mayoral banquets, City Livery Companies and stately homes.

The film is loosely based on the life of Ramsay MacDonald, Labour's first Prime Minister, and its most celebrated (or notorious) turncoat. The narrative, on the face of it, is framed by great events. It proceeds in the form of a chronicle, the entire screen being given up to significant dates. In the first place, there is Peterloo, the massacre of 1819 which provides the young Hamer Lockwood with his warrior vision, as well as with the sabre or sword which his grandfather had captured from the Manchester yeomanry. Then the heroic days of what used to be referred to as 'The Labour Pioneers'. Later the Suffragette agitation, which moves Hamer's wife courageously to take up arms against him, and has her force-fed in prison for her pains; then the Great War, in which Hamer turns himself into a patriot-recruiter, attempting to browbeat the Welsh miners back to work; finally, the Great Betrayal of 1931, and the nemesis inflicted on its architect by the class whom he deserted — the constituents who finally turn on Hamer. But, for all these nominal highlights, it is the domestic relations of Labour which preoccupy the film-makers, translating the issues of high politics into those of personal loyalties: character is the real subject of the drama; the events are a mere backdrop to the meeting and parting of friends.

57

Politically and imaginatively the film owes as much to Lancashire liberalism as it does to British socialism. Social divisions are conceptualised in terms of rich and poor rather than of workers and employers; politics is a choice between 'principles' and power. Land is the metaphor of exploitation, and the class enemy is the landlord, rather than the factory master; both the slum landlords who squeeze the people for their rents and the great territorial magnates who ride on their great estates. In Hamer's encounter with a gamekeeper, the point at which the film suggests the iron enters into his soul, there is more than an echo of the land campaigns of Lloyd George and their Chamberlainite predecessor, the 'Unauthorised Programme' of 1885. The insistent reference to Peterloo takes us back to an earlier phase of Liberalism, one which pitted the hand-loom weavers of the Pennines against the Parson and the Squire, and it is the cry of that time, 'Bread and Liberty', which propels the young Hamer on a lifetime's political career.

Like any good fiction, *Fame Is the Spur* (the film if not the novel) plays fast and loose with the facts of history. An opening sequence has a street corner orator spouting the message of socialism at a time (1877) when British socialism, as an organised movement, was yet unborn; while the Manchester bookseller, where Hamer serves as a junior, sports a photograph of Karl Marx at a time (1880) when none of the great man's works had been translated. Hamer is made a firebrand in his youth, where MacDonald was more of a wirepuller; he bends to the Jingo fever in 1914, where MacDonald (disconcertingly for subsequent Labour demonologies) courageously stood out. Finally, it credits Hamer with government office in 1927, at a time of Tory rule. But on the substance of the matter the film-makers, like Howard Spring, seem to have an intuitive feel for the Labour pioneers, and the circumstances in which the crusade was launched — first, to public indifferences and disbelief but, later, commanding the deepest loyalties. The peculiar social complexion of the early Independent Labour Party is nicely caught, not so much a working class Party, but rather a movement of the idealistic young, uniting the elementary school teacher, the rebellious young shopmen, the artistically-minded clerk with the self-educated working man. Particular attention is paid, quite rightly, to the well-born or well-educated converts to the cause, many of them, in the idiom of the day, 'ladies' — princesses as they appeared to Labour's love-lorn young bachelors, and on the ILP platforms, as in *Fame Is the Spur*, the ideal carriers of Labour's spiritual values. The cross-class romance which linked such rising stars of the ILP as the young Ramsay MacDonald and Philip Snowden to well-born consorts (MacDonald went into deep and very public mourning when his wife died), is here finely represented in the marriage of Michael Redgrave and Rosamund John, and the film convincingly shows how politics served as a higher plane on which the discomforts of social class were suspended.

The film, in the manner of 1940s 'social conscience' cinema (*The Stars Look Down* and *The Citadel* would be other examples, as also, arguably, the misleadingly-titled *Millions Like Us*) is unashamedly *paternalist*, and here too, one might suggest, it was intuitively in sympathy with Labour. The working class are the objects of social reform, and for the most part a silent army of sufferers, mute witnesses at the rich man's feast. Care-worn and work-weary, like Hamer's mill-girl mother, or his early supporters in the constituency, they wait for deliverance from on high. Arnold, the Labour organiser, is a shepherd with his flock, anxious to curb their excesses, solicitous for their welfare. Hamer, though sprung from the working class, is every inch a gentleman, even if he does not contrive to appear — as Ramsay MacDonald did in his years of glory — an aristocrat to the manner born. Rosamund John is both an Edwardian 'New Woman' and a lady, while her aunt, a Labour 'Left' as well as an intransigent suffragette, is an aristocratic eccentric of the kind whom Margaret Rutherford delighted to represent on the Silver Screen. The working class, by contrast, remain a sullen mass and indeed incipiently a mob as in the election riot which marks Hamer's first electoral contest. The one exception to this, a working class who are credited with the political consciousness and also (as in other British films of the period) dignified by being represented by a male voice choir, are the Welsh miners, who are given a crucial place in the drama.

Arnold, Hamer's *alter ego*, is the personification of Labour's ideal virtues. Modest and unassuming, he has a quiet line in self deprecation and an intuitive understanding of the essentially apolitical character of his following. Eschewing histrionics, of the kind which carry Hamer to the Valhalla of national fame, he yet keeps faith, standing by the colliers when they are out on strike, leading them in the Hunger March which Hamer dares not meet. He doesn't aspire to office, or pretend to political understanding, but his principles stand him in good stead, protecting him from the Jingo fever in 1914, and propelling him, in the aftermath of the General Strike, to stand up for the locked-out miners. Indeed, in the contrast between Hamer and Arnold — the one glamorous, swashbuckling but congenitally unreliable, the other moderate and unheroic, but patient and unflagging in his commitment to the cause — it does not seem fanciful to suggest a re-enactment of that well-advertised personality clash which led Attlee, the 'little man' incarnate, to triumph in the election of 1945 over Churchill, the warrior-hero.

I chose *Fame Is the Spur* initially because it seemed to me, drawing on childhood memory (I first saw the film as a boy of 12), that it illustrated the Labour faith in which Raymond Williams, in common with tens of thousands of others of his generation, was reared, and which he always in some way retained, however much he transcended Labourism in other spheres — in particular the loathing of careerism and the fear of (which was also a fascination with) the aristocratic embrace. All this is something, it might be suggested, which Raymond himself spent half a lifetime at Cambridge fighting off. Seeing the film again suggests other affinities with Raymond's work, and the ways in which he conceptualised politics in terms of personal loyalties. Particularly striking, both as a key to the Labour imagination in 1945, and to that of Williams in his own chosen roots, is the enormous importance attached to the Welsh miners — as vivid a presence in *Fame Is the Spur* as in those more famous films and novels of the period such as *The Stars Look Down* and *How Green*

Was My Valley. The Welsh miners are at once the ultimate symbolic victims of injustice, and the most steadfast of Labour's constituencies. The issues at stake in the film — the rival claims of 'principle' and personal preferment, of morality and expediency — are those which exercised Raymond continuously in his political writings. They are also there in the form of the *Bildungsroman*, which he adopted not only for his Welsh trilogy (charting the progress of a poor boy from Pandy) but also in the magnificent fiction which he made of his own life — a kind of *Fame Is the Spur* in reverse — refusing identification with the higher-ups among whom he moved, and cleaving determinedly both to his real and his imaginary roots.

Howard Spring, whose novel is the substantial basis of the film, is a writer who would repay the historian's attention, far more so one might suggest — if one were interested in the imaginative underpinnings of Labour's victory in 1945 — than those 'Thirties' writers and poets who seem to monopolise the attention of the literary critics and anthologists. Like A.J. Cronin, whose social fictions have enjoyed a vigorous media afterlife in *Dr Finlay's Casebook*, he was a best-selling author on the railway bookstalls, and a favourite on the lending library circuit, as well as a source of cinema screenplays. Certainly if one were interested in the sources of Labour idealism or, in the case of *Fame Is the Spur*, Labour mythologies, these novels seem representative of the common currency of Labour or Labour-sympathising beliefs — as well as (like *Love on the Dole*) influential ambassadors of Labour's message.

One insight of this film — it is also a sub-theme in Raymond Williams's *Border Country*, with its contrast between Morgan Prosser, the disappointed militant who founds a Valleys business, and Harry Price (modelled on Raymond's own father), a railwayman who stays loyal to the cause — is of the affinity, as a form of self-expression or as a means of escape, between labour agitation and back-street enterprise. Here we are introduced to Hamer's other *alter ego*, Tom Hannaway (interestingly played by Bernard Miles, adding here the *chutzpah* or guile of a wide boy to his normal persona as an upright son of toil). Tom begins life as a back-street profiteer, trading in rats as a boy; later, he enters into partnership with Hamer as a fruit seller, and later still, matching Hamer's progress step-by-step, he blossoms into a self-made businessman and Conservative MP. As a stuffed shirt, in one of the closing sequences of the film, he is the sardonic witness to Hamer's collapse. It is an alternative version of the poor boy making good, and the film has the wit to see that this was one of Hamer's possible worlds, not only in principle, but as a real life stage in his rake's progress.

One of the interesting things about this film, by comparison with costume drama today, is its seemingly effortless realism. Inaccurate it may be or careless in point of detail but, believing passionately in its own narrative, the film seems neither overawed nor embarrassed by its chosen settings. They certainly look authentic, with the solitary exception of a Swiss dreamscape, where Hamer's wife is dying of TB. The slum on which the film opens is not a Gothic horror but an immediately recognisable and quite homely working-class interior; the Labour halls, where the socialist message is preached, are very much like those I remember in my Communist Party childhood. And it may be that this is a clue to the film's enduring strengths — a realism that was the result not so much of aesthetic choice but rather of historical proximity. In the Britain, and not least the London, of 1947, so much of late Victorian England was still in place, even hegemonic, that it required no suspension of disbelief to re-enact it. In a country where there were still 800,000 miners, and where the Rhonda valleys were lined from end to end with pit-shafts, it cannot have been difficult to imagine the pit village where Hamer, in an incendiary mood, carries his Peterloo sword. Likewise in a Britain where the 'two nations' remained in their imaginative fastnesses, and where the social gulfs were never more apparent than in the attempts to fraternise across the class divides, the film did not need to labour its point about the social question as the stuff of political drama. At the other end of the social scale, with the comfortable classes or the 'educated' enjoying, according to their own lights, a monopoly of culture while regarding working-class pleasures as by definition 'cheap', the film had no difficulty in portraying the lives of the rich as glamorous — as indeed for the narrative of the film they had to be if Hamer was to be drawn to them, as a moth to the glittering light. In a society where so far as manners and morals were concerned, if not material possessions, an *ancien régime* was still intact (consider the way it is played out in Noël Coward's film *In Which We Serve*), it did not seem fanciful to treat the divisions of rich and poor as ageless, the warranty for one of the central conceits of the film, the belief that 'Bread and Liberty' was an ancestral working-class cry.

Fame Is the Spur does not give us history, it gives us Labour mythology, very largely one — if my argument is correct — which had been inherited from its Liberal-Radical predecessors. Its moralities — with their deep suspicion of Vanity Fair and contempt for faint hearts and backsliders — those of the *Pilgrim's Progress*. Its narrative is the 'rags to riches' story seen from the angle of those who were left behind.

Even by the standards of Labour, though, a Party which in 1945 (as at other times in its history) made a virtue of its moderation, it is a very understated film. It passes lightly over the corruptions of power, treating them rather as an aberration of Hamer Lockwood than as systemic, and indeed we see none of his fellow collaborators in treachery to the cause. As a result, the Great Betrayal of 1931 is robbed of its terrors; a mere incident in the rake's progress rather than a remembered trauma. It is both a strength of the film and a weakness that Michael Redgrave, playing Hamer, is never allowed to lose his dignity. He is not the Judas figure betraying his followers in their hour of need, nor yet a monster of vanity and conceit. He does not even contrive to seem pitiably alone, in the closing scene of the film where he wrestles, unavailingly, with the Peterloo sword, attempting to wrench it free from its scabbard. His good looks are imperturbable, his widowhood untroubled. He remains at the end of the film, as he is in his bookshop apprenticeship, little more than an ambitious political on the make. L. MacNeil Weir, Ramsay MacDonald's erstwhile secretary, devoted a whole book to the fallen idol and titled it a 'tragedy'. It is an angry book, but also in the end an illuminating one, painting a portrait of a man intoxicated by the power of words and yet fuddled by the cloudiness of belief. Unusually, it gives due credit to MacDonald's baffled idealism, as a war resister in the dire circumstances of 1914-18. Here one sees, as it were, Hamer and Arnold rolled into one, a dialectical clash of values taking place within the same breast rather than assigned to opposing figureheads. As a human drama I find it more convincing than any fiction. Perhaps some British film-maker would consider taking it up.

In Labour mythology, Ramsay MacDonald is the cuckoo in the nest, one who revealed his true colours in the Great Betrayal of 1931. Purged of his presence, the legend used to run (in the days when Labour's history could be portrayed as a 'magnificent journey'), the Party returned to the fold. In fact, it was a substantially new Party which emerged, one shorn not only of MacDonald and Snowden, its erstwhile leaders, but also of the Independent Labour Party, the 'conscience' of the movement, which seceded in the following year, albeit moving to the Left rather than to the Right. The new Party, as it emerged from the electoral defeat of 1931, was ruled by trade union and big city bosses (Ernest Bevin, of the Transport Workers Union, later a Labour Foreign Minister, and Herbert Morrison of the London Labour Party, later a Labour Home Secretary, are the representative figures). Labour loyalism, rather than ethical socialism, became the Party's working ideology; and planning — a term virtually unknown in Britain before 1931 — the Party's grand specific for poverty and unemployment.

This sea-change, which to this day is largely ignored by historians, can speculatively be put down to a concurrence of different causes: the devastating influence of the slump, in the wake of the Wall Street crash of 1929; the rise of economic nationalism — a pan-European phenomenon of the 1930s; the success, or seeming success, of the Soviet Five Year Plans (in 1932 not only the Webbs, but half the Labour leadership, it seemed — among them the architect of its planning policies, Hugh Dalton — had taken themselves off on a pilgrimage to Russia). It was reinforced by the Left turn, in the early 1930s, of such technocratically-minded intellectuals as the scientists, the architects and the economists, who in later years, in such groups as the XYZ Club, were to provide the personnel for Labour's Think-Tanks. The advent of controls, under the Coalition government — the 'war socialism' of 1940-1945 — made it hegemonic. But it was MacDonald's defection which was the catalyst. It discredited, at a stroke, that high-flown rhetoric, compounded of ethical uplift and moral idealism which MacDonald and Snowden had practised so dazzlingly on the public platform, and which nourished Labour activism at the grassroots. It undermined the Party's universalism which had made it the anti-war Party in British politics — the neo-pacifism which was one of the substantial legacies of the Great War and the basis for MacDonald's popularity as Party leader (in the eyes of the rank-and-file, his opposition to the war in 1914-18, and his success as a disarmament negotiator in the Labour government of 1924, outweighed the apparent indirection of his more domestic politics). Whereas the Labour Party of the 1920s, like its ILP predecessors, was universalist, in the 1930s it turned to that social version of 'Little Englandism' which has remained the unofficial ideology of the Party to this day (the rise of the Labour Left in the 1930s, and the growth of the Communist Party, in either case on issues of foreign policy, provides negative testimony for this turn).

It seems possible that MacDonald's particular version of Nature-worship, which had so captivated working-class audiences (no speech, it sometimes seemed, was complete without some visionary reference to his wanderings in the Highland glens) was discredited too. It was common currency in the first generation of British socialists, a substantial legacy of William Morris and the Arts and Crafts movement. It was the grand inspiration of the Clarion League, the mass organisation of cyclists (in the Edwardian years they numbered 40,000) who on Sundays abandoned the towns and cities to preach the message of socialism on the village greens. It had also left its mark on Labour's practical policies, where the provision of swimming-baths for the slums ('Lansbury's Lidos' as they were derisorily called when, as Minister of Works in the 1929-31 government, he built them in Regent's Park), open-air nurseries (of the kind pioneered by Margaret MacMillan in Deptford) and the building of cottage housing were designed to bring the country into the city. Whereas in the 1920s Labour municipalities had been building cottage estates (most famously in the 'beautification of Bermondsey', where an ambitious Labour Council planted some 20,000 trees), in the new dispensation, as practised by Morrison at the Labour LCC, and Leeds Labour Council at Quarry Hill, it was associated with the building of 'workers' flats', monuments to the slum clearance schemes of the 1930s, but also the remote ancestors of Labour's 1960s tower blocks.

As a Labour morality, fashioned in the shadow of the Party's 1945 victory, *Fame Is the Spur* could hardly be expected to take account of this, but at the risk of pedantry one might point to the falsifications which its narrative (and filmic) simplicities entailed. Hamer is no longer a tribune of the people, intoxicated by his own rhetoric, nor, like the real-life young MacDonald, a practitioner of 'New Life' ideals (one of the bonds between MacDonald and Margaret Ethel MacDonald, his wife). Hamer is a mere self-seeker, a Joe Lampton *avant la lettre* rather than a pilgrim who lost his way. His dalliances with aristocracy — unlike MacDonald's association with the Marchioness of Londonderry, a passionate if Platonic affair — are as calculated as his espousal of poverty's cause. MacDonald's persona as a 'countryman' — one of the invisible bonds which drew him to Stanley Baldwin, his Conservative counterpart, long before they joined hands at the head of the National government — is ignored. So too is his self-appointed role as a peacemaker, something which won him overwhelming support in his landslide electoral victory of 1931 as it was to do — if rather more briefly — for Neville Chamberlain in the period of Munich and 'appeasement'.

The Corn Is Green

A drama of a 'scholarship boy' from the Welsh mining valleys of a previous generation to Raymond Williams, and one with a very different politics. A play by Emlyn Williams, based on his own boyhood, and in the film version dominated by Bette Davis as the village schoolmistress, fighting off the attentions of the village 'slut' so that her chosen hero — a miner's son — can make it to university.

The Tree of Wooden Clogs and 'People of The Black Mountains'

Jenny Uglow

The dignity of ordinary lives, the pressure of outside events on remote communities, the legacy of a vanished past and, above all, the power of place — these are some of the themes which link Raymond Williams's novels to Ermanno Olmi's film —*L'Albero degli zoccoli*, better known in English as *The Tree of Wooden Clogs.*

After many years in which I had been strongly influenced by Raymond Williams's work, I first met him in the 1980s when, as editor at The Hogarth Press, I worked on the paperback reissues of his criticism and fiction. (The three novels which make up his trilogy *Border Country*, *Second Generation* and *The Fight for Manod*, which he had long wanted to see back in print, were reissued in the week of his death in January 1988.) At the moment I am involved in the publication of his last novel *People of the Black Mountains*, set in the beautiful area of Wales, facing the English border, where Williams himself grew up. The region forms the background to all his fiction, but this latest, extraordinary work brings to life (in over 250,000 words) the experiences of the different peoples of the mountains not over one or two lifetimes but over thousands of generations.[1]

People of the Black Mountains is a chronicle with a difference. It is framed within the night-long quest of a young man for his grandfather, who has vanished during a walk on the high ridges. When Glyn reaches the heights the rhythms of his body change. He hears a voice calling within him and suddenly we are pulled back through the millennia: to Marod and his family, sheltering in the great caves, hunting wild horses in a misty arctic summer before the last Ice Age. As Glyn moves from place to place, sequences of stories form a linking chain across the ages, from 27,000 B.C. to

1415 A.D. Williams intended to bring the novel up to the present day, but sadly he died before this was accomplished.

Could there, I wondered when this film season was suggested, possibly be a film like this? The answer was no, not exactly. One could look to British film and television for parallels with Williams's earlier fiction: *Border Country* suggests *My Ain Folk*; *Second Generation* has much in common with the grainy, realistic, regional and political cinema of the 1950s and 60s; *A Fight for Manod* can be linked to more recent films like *Local Hero*. But to find anything which shared the same atmosphere as *Black Mountains* we had to look abroad, to films like Umberto Lenzi's ambitious, if unsuccessful *La Guerra del ferro* (*Quest for Fire*), to the Chinese *Yellow Earth*, or even to the magical-realist genres of Central and South America. Williams's novel, so rooted in Welsh soil, came to seem a peculiarly un-British work.

In the end, after much discussion with friends, I chose *The Tree of Wooden Clogs* (1978) even though its time-span — a few months at the end of the last century — differs greatly from that of *Black Mountains*. It is a naturalistic portrayal of the lives of peasant families in the Bergamo region who live together in a *cascina*, a communal holding owned by a landlord, and the events are those of daily life — the birth of a child, the slaughter of a pig, the harvest, a wedding trip, a cow's sickness. In a different way from the novel the film is also composed of interlinking stories, in which the personal dramas of each family blend into the larger story of the community as a whole. One crucial incident gives the film its title: the priest tells the peasant Batisti that his eldest son should go to school, but on his way home one day, his son, Minek, breaks one of his clogs. Shoes are essential for the long walk to school and education is the chance of a better life, so to make a new clog Batisti chops down one of his landlord's trees. When the act is discovered the whole family is evicted. As they leave, their fellow peasants, with whom they have shared their life, look on with despair and sympathy but make no open protest.

Like Williams's novel, Olmi's film neither patronises nor idealises its subjects. It is elegiac, but not nostalgic, and although it makes no direct political statement its clear picture of exploitation invites our anger and suggests that the social order must be challenged: despite the passivity of the rural workers' resistance, change will come. Like Williams in his previous novels, Olmi works in a tradition of realism but the cumulative effect of the dull earth colours — yellows, greens and ochres — the centrally placed images and the careful choice of sounds — church bells, Bach organ and cello music, the travelling pipers at Christmas — give it great resonance and emotional power.

Ermanno Olmi has been described as the Italian film-maker most identified with and committed to a particular regional heritage. The preoccupation with a specific region, in both Olmi and Williams, stems primarily from a deep loyalty and love of the area in which they grew up. Their involvement leads them to question the way most social, political and historical analyses tend to omit local experiences which don't fit general definitions, to ignore complex tensions within nations, and to gloss over the way that 'history' moves at a different pace in different places. But although both men return continuously to this theme in their work, their treatment of it is complicated (and in some ways confused) by a strong autobiographical element — the abstract issue of regionalism can't be separated entirely from their own ambivalent responses to their childhood and their inheritance.

Olmi was born in the Bergamo district; Williams was born in the Black Mountains. Both men, in a real sense, are dramatising their own history, the collective memory of their forebears. They know the land and its people intimately. Both men, too, leave, then return to, their native land after excursions into very different territories. Williams's earlier novels deal with tension between a Welsh past and the demands of wider events in the present. In *Border Country*, a young man visits his dying father and discovers his own identity while remembering his childhood, the impact of the General strike on the small village and the events leading up to his departure for university. In *Second Generation*, Welsh families have crossed the border to work in an industrial university town in England where they are caught in a mesh of political, cultural and sexual turmoil. In *The Fight for Manod* the heroes of the two previous novels meet and return to Wales, this time to deal with the onslaught of Westminster and international capital, in the shape of plans to flood a remote valley.

In a similar way, the films Olmi made before *Wooden Clogs* treat the clash of rural and urban cultures and the pull of a regional background: the moment of contact between two men of different generations, one from the South, the other from the North, guarding a dam in *Il tempo si è fermato*; the bewilderment of a young man from the country facing industrial life in *Il posto*; the problems of a worker moving out of his region in *I fidanzati*; the return of a prisoner of war to his native village in *I recuperanti*.

In his fiction, Raymond Williams acknowledges his own separation by the device of a young man returning to the land of his fathers (and grandfathers). There is no such intermediary in *Wooden Clogs* but Olmi's film grew from stories told him by his own grandfather and he has explained that he had wanted to make it for twenty years; 'the film is really a story of my childhood, stories that have long lived in my memory crying to be told'[2] — much as the stories in *Black Mountains* cry out within Glyn's mind and demand to be heard. Both writer and film-maker are interested in the different kinds of knowledge held by the older generation who remain in the country, and the younger generation who leave. In the novel, Glyn reflects on the contrasting approaches to local history of his grandfather Elis, a telephone engineer with a detailed knowledge of the mountains and passionate love of their history, and his father, Elis's son, a brilliant academic historian. While the books which Elis reads so voraciously may not always be correct, does the keen-eyed scrutiny of professionals necessarily lead to a more accurate kind of history?

Pushing away, often coldly, the enthusiasms of the amateur, they would reduce what they were studying to an internal procedure; in the worst cases to material for an enclosed career. If lives and places were being seriously sought, a

> powerful attachment to lives and places was entirely demanded. The polystyrene
> model and its textual and theoretical equivalents remained different from the
> substance which they reconstructed and simulated. Only the breath of the place,
> its winds and its mouths, stirred the model into life.[3]

Olmi presents his view of history more obliquely. In his film the time
is the present, yet the life we see is rooted in a long past, and our
response to it is affected by what we know of the future to come.
Since the 1950s, when he made over forty short documentaries of
industrial life for Edison, Olmi's work has started from the
observation of ordinary life. His initial impetus was not theoretical or
aesthetic but emotional: 'I began by taking pictures of objects and
people sheerly for the love of them. Shooting these pictures also was
a way of coming closer to the world of work that I shared with my
colleagues.'[4] His characters rarely reflect on what happens to them
and the knowledge of elderly people, like Anselmo, the grandfather
in *Wooden Clogs*, is not analytical but intuitive and practical, born of
a long life. He attributes his portrayal of this kind of tacit knowledge
to the influence of his own grandmother.

> I spent many years living with my grandmother, a peasant woman of great
> wisdom (not scholastic wisdom but the fruit of a life lived with utter
> clearsightedness). As a result I feel a great deal of tenderness towards such old
> sages.[5]

In keeping with this concern for unknown lives, Olmi's actors were
all amateurs, local people chosen after he spent months living in the
village. They worked from no definite script but from a sequence of
scenes: the action and dialogue came from the actors themselves. Yet
despite the naturalism, we know that the story is fiction and the film
has a sense of self-enclosure, as if we observe rather than share the
experiences shown. There is an analogy to our position within the
film, in a scene where the landlord (who enjoys playing opera on his
new gramophone, an invention which astonishes the peasants) peers
through a barred window and watches his wife listen to a young man
playing the piano. He is cut off from the peasants by his role as
landlord, and, in a different way, he is also distanced from the music
which his records recreate. A modern audience, watching the film, is

similarly excluded from the life on the screen, separated first by time and class and second by the artifice of cinema itself.

Williams and Olmi deliberately make use of fictional genres, with an implicit acknowledgement of their subjectivity, because they want to focus on people who find no place in 'objective' histories: the boy Aron, for example, in *Black Mountains*, who tries to tether a pig, much to the amusement of the rest of his stone-age hunting settlement. Aron's attempt fails, but, says Williams, it would probably be repeated, failing or succeeding intermittently, hundreds of times over the next 2000 years before the great change from hunting to herding and cultivation finally took place. We now see the past, foreshortened, as epochs, but in reality the pace is always local and day to day.

The characters in Williams's novel and Olmi's film are also marginalised in conventional historical accounts because from their point of view the most important events are local, while standard histories take broader national or European frames. Wales becomes subsumed under Britain or, even worse, under 'England'; Bergamo at the turn of the century is part of a relatively new Italian nation. Both novel and film resist these wider patterns, which, they suggest, falsify the experience of individual lives. Thus, as Williams points out, the Roman account of their invasions identified the diverse and the fiercely contending tribes as 'Britons', regardless of their local identity and the fact that the ruling warrior class were a different race from their subject people. The next step was to make a wider grouping still, linking them with other races who shared similar languages and cultures, and describing them all as 'Celts'. And although they had never seen it this way themselves, the Celts would eventually adopt this Roman version of a central identity and use it in their own legends of resistance, as something they had lost.

In the story sequences of *Black Mountains* we see how myths, legends and accounts of events like the coming of plague or invasions are carried through the ages and interpreted by story-tellers before they are collected into written history, and, more importantly, how this version of history may differ from that later seen as authoritative. In *Wooden Clogs* a session story-telling in the barn on a stormy evening still expresses the peasants' own view of their position — as in Batisti's gripping tale of a rich woman's ghost who gets her own back on a thief who has cut off her hand to steal a ring (in other words, there is no way the poor can beat the bourgeoisie, even when they're dead).[6]

The sense of local and class identity is further emphasised by language. The first version of *Wooden Clogs* was made in the Bergamese dialect, later dubbed in Italian for the general market. Beneath the English of *Black Mountains* lie traces of many languages, like the arrowheads still in the soil: Celtic, Latin, Saxon, medieval Welsh, Norman French — their layers reflecting waves of invasion, domination, submission, oppression.

Yet, although the foreground of both film and novel is personal, communal and regional and the basic rhythms are those of the land and the seasons, this is not the whole picture. The life of the communities are affected, directly or indirectly, by the general upheavals of society, and the people are caught up in eddies of change: political, economic, technological. As *Black Mountains* traces the long, slow transition, over thousands of years, from herding settlements to feudal baronies, Williams shows us how the rules which govern communities develop. At first they come from within, as mechanisms of survival — like the ice-age hunters' custom of exposing girl babies in times of hardship, to keep the number of mouths down and to maintain the proportion of male hunters. But gradually such rules become objectified, transformed into systems with their own rationale, imposed from without — by religious orders like the Druids, by the Romans, by the Norman overlords. Although at their height such social systems come to seem 'natural' to the population at large, they operate in the interests of particular groups and each in turn is either modified, or openly defied, as conditions change.

Wooden Clogs depicts a period in which the economic, political and religious systems are so entrenched, and their hierarchies so dominant, that the peasants' loss of control over their lives seems absolute — the landlord takes two-thirds of the produce, the workers are valued solely for their labour, their assault on his property is cruelly punished. But the landlord is only part of a larger network of control which is, in fact, already being challenged. At their marriage, a gentle young couple are warned by the priest against 'silly ideas' circulating abroad. On a wedding journey to Milan they see from their barge on the river a pall of smoke on the horizon, and hear talk of troops and demonstrators. As soon as they arrive in the city a line of shuffling prisoners blocks their way, and they have to shelter in doorways from mounted soldiers racing through the streets: apparently a reference to 'the notorious street battle of 1898 in which General Bava Beccaris ordered his troops to charge on an unarmed crowd and massacred fifty people'.[7] Although they do not understand the significance of what they see, we feel that the turmoil now affecting the industrial workers will in time touch the life of the country as well.

A key figure of authority in Olmi's film, at least as important as the landlord, is Don Carlo, the priest. Religion permeates every aspect of the peasants' existence and Olmi's uncritical treatment of the grip of the Catholic church has alienated some socialist commentators. Faith is presented as a consoling, binding element, part of the culture, enshrining mysteries beyond the mundane. Its central place in life is embodied in episodes like that where the widow Runk fetches holy water to heal her sick cow. Her desperately muttered prayers are a last resort, a personal appeal to Christ: 'Without your help we'll never survive...You can't refuse'.

The widow's faith can be seen as superstition, springing from despair, but elsewhere the message of the gospels is shown to inspire compassion and responsibility: the children are reprimanded for laughing at the village idiot because 'those who are wretched are nearer to God'; the Mother Superior says 'If we don't help each other, no-one will help us'. Christian resignation may be a factor in the peasants' passivity, but it is also a bond of solidarity, and it does not preclude criticism or recognition of the urgent need for change. Olmi (who had already made several documentaries for the Italian television channel, RAI) offers that problematic combination — 'a traditionalist Christian committed to the highest aspirations of Marxism'.[8]

Raymond Williams too has to confront the place of religion in the lives of ordinary people over the centuries, from the varied beliefs and sacred places of hunter and herdsman to the coming of Christendom. But his approach, very different from Olmi's, is that of an enquiring humanist who understands the need for faith and the binding power of ritual but who seeks to explain them in terms of the conditions of material life. Even when dealing with early religions, he separates the mystical elements from the power and vested interests of the institutions, showing the processes by which religious orders become increasingly remote from, and exploitative of, the labouring people. But both men, even the more conservative Olmi, recognise the way that a need for hope, for some belief in a power beyond the natural and the human, can be used to validate an oppressive social order.

The small communities in *People of the Black Mountains* struggle to survive natural disasters and to keep their individual identity through wave after wave of territorial struggles. *The Tree of Wooden Clogs* depicts a handful of families on a single Italian estate at the turn of the century, whose way of life has vanished under the impact of the twentieth century. The work of Williams and Olmi is grounded in theory, but their aim is not analysis so much as imaginative re-creation of the past. Both men use their chosen medium to depict continuity and change, culture and politics from the perspective of a particular place and both raise a neglected issue for socialists — how literature, art and theory have dealt, and should deal, with the question of regionalism and local culture. In doing so, they ask their readers and audiences to look again at the way 'history' is experienced, the way it is recorded, and the way it is judged and interpreted today.

(Unfortunately, *The Tree of Wooden Clogs* was unavailable for the NFT season.)

NOTES

1. The novels of Raymond Williams are *Border Country* (1960, Hogarth Press paperback 1988), *Second Generation* (1964, p/bk 1988), *The Volunteers* (1978, p/bk 1985), *The Fight for Manod* (1979, p/bk 1988) and *Loyalties* (1987, p/bk 1989). *People of the Black Mountains* will be published in two parts. The first, 'The Beginning', will appear in September 1989; the second, provisionally entitled 'The Eggs of the Eagle', in 1990.
2. *Newsweek*, June 4, 1979.
3. *People of the Black Mountains*, typescript.
4. C. Samuels, *Encountering Directors*, (1972) p109, quoted by Michael B. Gladych in *Film Quarterly*, Winter 1980/81.
5. Samuels, ibid, p100.
6. R.T. Whitcombe, *The New Italian Cinema*, (1982) p195.
7. Jonathan Keates, *Sight and Sound*, Winter 1988/9.
8. R. McCormick, *Cineaste*, ix, no. 4, 1979.

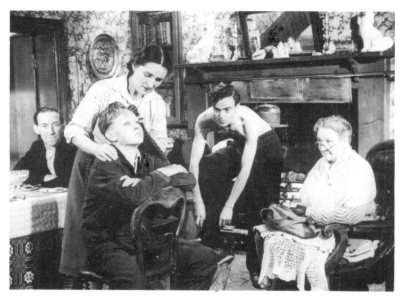

Blue Scar: Family Politics

Daniel: Politics at work, in the street

This Sporting Life: Rachel Roberts, late, in Serious England

Valley of Song: Rachel Roberts, early, in Comic Wales

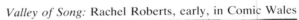

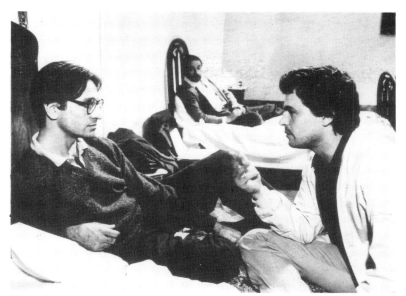

Three Brothers: in European Art Cinema

Z Cars: Policemen in British Popular Television

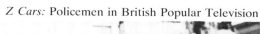

The Herd: Off the rails in the Third World

Paris, Texas: On the road in the First World

Paisà

Jim Cook

'1943-44. After the Allied invasion of Sicily, a US Infantry sergeant leaves Carmela, his patrol's guide, in a ruined coastal fortress. Trying to bridge the language barrier, her guard Joe is shot by a sniper while holding a light to a family photo. Germans occupy the fort and kill Carmela, who has hidden the dying Joe and then fired his rifle. The returning Americans find Joe's body and curse the girl.

In Naples, an orphaned boy 'steals' a drunken black MP and takes his boots. Three days later, the MP collars the boy; but, seeing his destitution, runs off, dropping the recovered boots.

Six months after the capture of Rome, Fred, a disillusioned tankman, talks drunkenly to a prostitute about how he was welcomed to the city by a girl named Francesca. The prostitute — Francesca — subsequently leaves and attempts unsuccessfully to arrange a replay of their first innocent rendezvous.

During the battle for Florence, an American nurse, Harriet, persuades an Italian, Massimo, to lead her across the Arno to find Lupo, an artist friend from before the war, now a legendary partisan. During a brief engagement, a partisan dies in Harriet's arms, muttering news of Lupo's death. The partisans summarily execute a group of Germans.

In a monastery in the Romagna, the monks are horrified that Bill Martin, a Roman Catholic padre, has not attempted to enlighten his companions, a Jew and a Protestant. Martin, however, is moved by the monks' serenity.

In the marshlands of the Po delta, a depleted band of partisans and American Special Services men fight a last-ditch stand. Caught by the Germans, the Italians are drowned, and Dale, one of the Americans, is summarily shot protesting the barbarity.' (*Monthly Film Bulletin*, November 1980.)

I don't know if Williams ever saw this film. There, are, however, intriguing correspondences between aspects of his life and concerns and the film which suggest it to me for inclusion in this tribute to him.

The War

Like others of his Left generation, like Edward Thompson, Richard Hoggart, Stuart Hood, and European counterparts, like Rossellini, Williams was indelibly marked by both the sheer local chaos of the war which the film expresses, and by that sense of a world forever changed.

'I don't think the intricate chaos of that Normandy fighting has ever been recorded. Everyone was mixed up, in front and behind each other, with all the time an appalling level of casualties. In one major offensive we were bombed by our own planes before we started. Virtually every day during the Normandy fighting we would see tanks like our own going up. That was the constant fear you lived with, confined within this little metal interior of the tank surrounded by hundreds of rounds of high-explosive ammunition and a considerable quantity of diesel fuel. If you got hit it was instant. I don't think that the situation would ever wholly have resolved itself, if it had not been that by sheer preponderance, as the Allied invasion built up, the Americans got round the back and the Germans had to pull out.

In that kind of fighting, what could you feel? You did not even know at times whether you were firing at your own troops or at others. Those were some of the worst experiences. Then on other occasions even the enemy lacked identity. Once a big attack was launched; we went in and made very substantial progress — when we looked around we had taken hundreds of prisoners. But they were Ukrainians and a whole mixture of other nationalities — there was hardly a German among them. This was a German tactic: they would put these troops in front and you would make six miles' progress.

80

Then the German units would be waiting for you much better armed. Some of these prisoners did not even know which country they were in. They really did not know who they were fighting...

The experience of the war was appalling. I don't think anybody really ever gets over it. First there is the guilt: about moments of cowardice, but also about moments of pure aggression and brutality. Are those really opposites? It is easy enough to feel guilty about when you felt frightened but much worse is the guilt once you've started recovering your full human perspective, which is radically reduced by the whole experiences of fighting...

An army functions as a true machine — the whole point of the training, although you don't realise it, is precisely to be able to do all these actions without being immediately motivated. You do in a battle what you did in an exercise, with, of course, much more chaos. What you lose is the most significant dimension of humanity — it is a commonplace about war, but is an absolute truth. You do function on a fighting animal level.' (*Politics & Letters* pp. 56-8. New Left Books 1979.)

Realism

Throughout his life Williams defined, refined and redefined his ideas around realism — the complex relations between forms of expression and their adequacy to social experience. Here, in a brilliantly lucid summary, he described the historical shifts of realism and, in so doing, provides for me a way into both the form of *Paisà* and of the world it describes.

'First there is a conscious movement towards social extension. There is a crucial argument in the early period of bourgeois tragedy about the need to extend the actions of tragedy from persons of rank, to whom by convention and precept tragedy had hitherto largely been confined, to — as it was put — "your equals, our equals". This movement of social extension — "let not your equals move your pity less" — is a key factor in what we can now identify as a realist intention. Then, second, there is a movement towards the siting of actions in the present, to making action contemporary. It is remarkable that in most preceding drama it seemed almost a constituent of dramatic form that it was set either in the historical or in a legendary past, and the emphasis on the actions of the contemporary world is the second defining feature of this new bourgeois realism. And the third, which is perhaps in the end the most important, is that there is an emphasis on secular action, in the quite precise sense that elements of the metaphysical or a religious order directly or indirectly frame, or in the stronger cases determine, the human actions within the earlier plays. This dimension is dropped, and in its place a human action is played through in specifically human terms — exclusively human terms. This was seen as a loss of significance, as a narrowing of drama. It is often condemned as a sentimentalisation of the tragic action, and indeed in local terms this was often true. But it is impossible to overlook the connection between this conscious secularisation and the development of attitudes which we must associate with realism in a much wider sense than that of dramatic methods, that is to say with the development of rationalism, of the scientific attitude, of historical attitudes towards society.' (From: 'A Lecture on Realism', *Screen*, Spring 1977, Vol 18, No.1.)

Differently expressed but not totally at variance with Williams is the involvement of the French critic and theorist André Bazin with realism and particularly with Italian Neo-Realism and the work of Rossellini. Bazin's writing on realism is as analogously complex as that of Williams precisely because of the reach of the connections that he also was trying to forge.

'Cinematographic styles can be grouped, though not in a hierarchy, in terms of the added reality they represent. We shall thus call *realist* any system of expression or narrative procedure tending to make more reality appear on the screen. Naturally 'reality' must not be understood in terms of quantity. The same event, the same object, is capable of several different representations. Each of them discards or retains some of the qualities that lead us to recognise the object on the screen, each of them introduces, to didactic or aesthetic ends, more or less corrosive abstractions which do not permit the original object to subsist in its entirety. At the end of this inevitable and necessary chemistry, an illusion of reality made up of a complex of abstraction (black-and-white, plane surface), of conventions, (the laws of montage for example) and of authentic reality has been substituted for the initial reality. It is a necessary illusion, but it leads rapidly to a loss of consciousness of reality itself, which is identified in the spectator's mind with its cinematographic representation...

The art of Rossellini consists of knowing how to give facts their densest and most elegant structure simultaneously; not the most gracious structure but the sharpest, most direct or more trenchant one. With him, neo-realism rediscovers naturally the style and the resources of abstraction. Respecting the real does not mean that you have to pile up appearances, on the contrary it means stripping it of everything that is not essential, it means attaining totality in simplicity. Rossellini's art seems linear and melodic. It is true that several of his films make one think of a sketch, the stroke indicates but does not paint....' (From: 'Bazin on Neo-Realism' by Christopher Williams [Williams's own translation], *Screen*, Winter 1973-4, Vol 14, No.4.)

'...The unit of cinematic narrative in *Paisà* is not the "shot", an abstract view of a reality which is being analysed, but the "fact". A fragment of concrete reality in itself multiple and full of ambiguity, whose meaning emerges only after the fact, thanks to other imposed facts between which the mind establishes certain relationships. Unquestionably, the director chose these "facts" carefully while at the same time respecting their factual integrity.' (From: 'An Aesthetic of Reality' by André Bazin in *What is Cinema Vol II*, University of California Press, 1971.)

Living on/Waiting/Persistence: Continuities

Here it might be objected that the greatest violence is being done to Williams and I am trying to forge connections that are not merely unorthodox but illegitimate. I can only argue that Williams's writing makes clearer for me, i.e. develops and extends, points that are expressed both by Rossellini himself and a sympathetic commentator on his work.

'*Paisà* showed two worlds coming into contact, each with its own psychology and spiritual outlook: the worlds of the victor and the vanquished. This contact gave rise to such confusion that in the end there were neither victors nor vanquished, only the day-to-day heroism of man in his attachment to life: living on, in spite of everything, whichever side he had been on.' (From: 'Rossellini on Rossellini', *Screen*, Winter, 1973-4, Vol 14, No.4.)

'*Paisà* is explicitly and implicitly suffused with the theme of waiting. According to Rossellini, the representation of waiting provides an ideal opportunity for reality to manifest itself in either real or fictitious time. In each episode of *Paisà*, someone is expecting an important event to take place, a hidden truth to become apparent, an anguish to disappear. The death of Carmela in the first episode puts an end to the confused emotions between her and the American soldier. In the final scene of the Neapolitan episode, which is built on hesitations, dreams and uncertainty, a black soldier finds himself in the worst shanty town he had ever seen. In the Roman episode, the GI tears up the piece of paper with the girl's address and thus marks the end of an illusion. The Florentine story, that of an anguished search, comes to an end when it is revealed that the man who the woman has been looking for is dead. The episode in the monastery focuses on tensions that build while protagonists wait for a common dinner, which the Italian monks will ultimately refuse to eat, deciding to fast for the salvation of the two non-Catholics. And the last episode is simply a waiting for death.

Continuity among the six episodes is established by newsreel footage and by the off-screen voice of a radio announcer covering the Allied advance into Italian territory. *Paisà* is not a chronicle of war events. Nor it is a cinematic Decameron — a collection of stories told by different people at a certain historical moment — as is so frequently the case in Italian literature and cinema. The film transcends mere authenticity of events by revealing unique human attitudes. In *Open City*, such attitudes were paradigmatic, but in *Paisà* they reach beyond the given fact. Rossellini's own anguish, desire and fears, which were later manifested in *Germany, Year Zero*, are already reflected in some of *Paisà*'s characters, who are photographed so as to appear as part of the landscape. They are almost never shown without their surroundings, as if imprisoned by the film's frame itself. The premise of Sartre's *Huis clos* has never been truer than in *Paisà*: there is no escape from the encounter with truth. Rossellini later observed:

> Usually, in the traditional film, a scene is composed as follows: a long shot, we see the milieu, the character, we approach it; then a medium shot, a three-quarter view, a close-up; and then the story of the character is told. I proceed in an opposite way: a person moves and his movements make us discover his surroundings. I begin always with a close-up; then the movements of the camera, as it follows the actor, reveal the milieu. The actor must never be left alone: he must move in a complex and comprehensive way.'

(From: *Passion & Defiance. Film in Italy from 1942 to the Present* by Mira Liehm, University of California Press, 1984.)

'The ideas and images of country and city retain their great force. This persistence has a significance matched only by the fact of the great actual variation, social and historical, of the ideas themselves. Clearly, the contrast of country and city is one of the major forms in which we become conscious of the central part of our experience and of the crises of our society. But when this is so, the temptation is to reduce the historical variety of the forms of interpretation to what are loosely called symbols or archetypes: to abstract even these most evidently social forms and to give them a primarily psychological or metaphysical status. This reduction often happens when we find certain major forms and images and ideas persisting through periods of great change. Yet if we can see that the persistence depends on the forms and images and ideas being changed, though often subtly, internally and at times unconsciously, we can see also that the persistence indicates some permanent or effectively permanent need, to which the changing interpretations speak. I believe that there is indeed such a need, and that it is created by the processes of a particular history. But if we do not see these processes, or see them only incidentally, we fall back on modes of thought which seem able to create the permanence without the history. We may find emotional or intellectual satisfaction in this, but we have then dealt with only half the problem, for in all such major interpretations it is the co-existence of persistence and change which is really striking and interesting, and which we have to account for without reducing either fact to a form of the other.' (From Chapter 25, 'Cities & Countries' in *The Country & The City* by Raymond Williams, Paladin, 1975.)

A Structure of Feeling

As a way of articulating his thoughts about persistence and change, Williams developed the notion of 'structures of feeling'. This is one of his most penetrating and again endlessly reworked concerns centring on 'forming and formative processes' rather than 'formed wholes' and aimed at keeping alive and dynamic the relations between experience and cultural activity.

In these final extracts he describes first the processes that move towards 'fixing' and then goes on to talk about the more nuanced possibilities of being alive to 'structures of feeling'. In so doing he highlights for me — maybe it's again an illegitimate use of Williams — *Paisà*'s extraordinary mix of conveying the immediacy of war's chaos along with a prescient anticipation of a world forever changed by both Fascism *and* America in Europe and waiting to be reformed anew and different. He illuminates, in other words, the film's realism in terms of both the immediacy it describes and the social experience it strives to understand and clarify.

'In most description and analysis, culture and society are expressed in an habitual past tense. The strongest barrier to the recognition of human cultural activity is this immediate and regular conversion of experience into finished products. What is defensible as a procedure in conscious history, where on certain assumptions many actions can be definitively taken as having ended, is habitually projected, not only into the always moving substance of the past, but into contemporary life, in which relationships, institutions and formations in which we are still actively involved are converted, by this procedural mode, into formed wholes rather than forming and formative processes...

The term structure of feeling is difficult, but 'feeling' is chosen to emphasise a distinction from more formal concepts of 'world-view' or 'ideology'. It is not only that we must go beyond formally held and systematic beliefs, though, of course, we have always to include them. It is that we are concerned with meanings and values that are actively lived and felt, and the relations between these and formal or systematic beliefs are in practice variable (including historically variable), over a range from formal assent with private dissent to the more nuanced interaction between selected and interpreted beliefs and acted and justified experiences. An alternative definition would be structures of experience: in one sense the better and wider word, but with the difficulty that one of its senses has that past tense which is the most important obstacle to recognition of the areas of social experience which is being defined. We are talking about characteristic elements of impulse, restraint and tone; specifically affective elements of consciousness and relationships: not feelings against thought, but thought as felt and feeling as thought: practical consciousness of a present kind, in a living and inter-relating continuity. We are, then, defining these elements as a 'structure': as a set with specific internal relations, at once interlocking and in tension. Yet we are also defining a social experience which is still in process, often indeed not yet recognised as social but taken to be private, idiosyncratic and even isolating, but which in analysis (though rarely otherwise) has its emergent, connecting and dominant characteristics, indeed its specific hierarchies. These are often more recognisable at a later stage, when they have been (as often happens) formalised, classified, and in many cases built into institutions and formations. By that time the case is different; a new structure of feeling will usually already have begun to form, in the true social present...

The hypothesis has a special relevance to art and literature, where the true social content is in a significant number of cases of this present and affective kind, which cannot without loss be reduced to belief-systems, institutions or explicit general relationships, though it may include all these as lived and experienced, with or without tension, as it also evidently includes elements of social and material (physical or natural) experience which may lie beyond, or be uncovered or imperfectly covered by, the elsewhere recognisable systematic elements. The unmistakable presence of certain elements in art which are not covered by (though in one mode they may be reduced to) other formal systems is the true source of the specialising categories of "the aesthetic", "the arts" and "imaginative literature". We need, on the one hand, to acknowledge (and welcome) the specificity of these elements — specific feelings, specific rhythms — and yet to find ways of recognising their specific kinds of sociality, thus preventing that extraction from social experience which is conceivable only when social experience itself has been categorically (and at root historically) reduced. We are then not only concerned with the restoration of social content in its full sense, that of a generative immediacy. The idea of a structure of feeling can be specifically related to the evidence of forms and conventions — semantic figures — which, in art and literature, are often among the first indications that such a new structure is forming.' (From: Chapter 9, 'Structures of Feeling' in *Marxism and Literature* by Raymond Williams, OUP, 1977.)

I'm no Williams scholar or expert, but over the years I guess I've used him in this simplifying, gadfly, collaging way. As the saying goes (and it's both a cliché and something I'm fundamentally grateful for) he makes me think, and rethink. Across these few pages his ideas and insights have allowed me to do this in relation to *Paisà*. I hope he wouldn't have objected.

A Generation

Ken Worpole

In 1959, at the age of 15, I joined the Labour Party Young Socialists in Hadleigh, Essex, and became embroiled for the next four years in going to meetings. Branch meetings, ward meetings, constituency meetings, caucus meetings, regional meetings, national conferences, study meetings, meetings to arrange meetings, meetings to report back from other meetings, and meetings called to censure people for not attending meetings. We met therefore we were. Perhaps a quarter of all these meetings made some contribution to political change; the other three-quarters were simply bad and unnecessary theatre: politics reduced to set speeches and exhortatory resolutions echoing in half-empty rooms in which the ash-trays were never emptied and the broken chairs never repaired. Yet I was lucky. For in the course of all this apparent activity and very little achievement I made some long-lasting friendships, and in the end what some of us got out of those years was not political change so much as ideas for the kinds of lives we wanted to lead and the world we wanted to live in.

For when we were not meeting we were enjoying ourselves, which is to say we were learning from each other rather than hectoring each other on things we barely understood. Sitting in each others' kitchens or front rooms late at night, listening to records, talking about books, planning demonstrations, falling in love, arranging trips to the cinema or what to do on Saturday night; we were, of course, no different from anybody else. Or were we? What I remember most strongly was the range of backgrounds that we variously came from: grammar school students, office workers, apprentices from Ford's, shop-workers, unemployed young people, council workers — sons and daughters of the middle class, sons and daughters of the workers. Quite a number had parents who were in the Labour Party or the Communist Party; the children of Quaker parents seemed more common than might have been expected. We wanted to change the world and we wanted something to do in the evenings.

In that period the world was palpably divided into two distinct power blocs: East and West. An iron curtain, and subsequently a large concrete and barbed wire wall, divided the two, and this division of the world exercised our imaginations, sympathies, fears and hopes, day and night. The Cold War was an ideological construct, but it was also a state of mind. The air was literally thick with it. 'Go back to Russia!' was a common rebuke to many of our proffered leaflets, doorstep enquiries or local pickets and demonstrations. The Cold War was fought out at the United Nations conference table, and in the brinkmanship of gunboat and airspace manoeuvres in the four corners of the world; it also tinged everyday life in urban Essex. Anti-communism was a dominant form of commonsense politics.

For the most part our political sympathies — and certainly our organisational forms! — were with and from the East, yet our emotions remained largely shaped in the West. Between the two great electrical poles of capitalism and communism, cultural processes and forms kept short-circuiting. We studied Lenin, but listened to Leadbelly; we went to lectures on democratic centralism then late at night tuned in to the AFN (American Forces Network) station broadcasting Willis Conover's *Jazz at Midnight* from Munich. (In Britain it was of course only 11 o'clock, one hour behind mainland Europe.) We organised regular minibus trips to the Theatre Royal at Stratford in East London where we saw the original productions of *The Quare Fellow* and *The Hostage*, and we thought that Irish folk music and Irish theatre were a direct inheritance of the British left, as also were novels translated from the French and Swedish films.

Yet somehow we could never square the political with the cultural, the one inescapably rigid, the other free-ranging and profuse; there was always something at odds with the two processes. I suppose exploring that disjuncture has been a large part of my subsequent intellectual life; I still love the idiosyncrasies and discordancies of

free-form jazz and yet I want a culture held and made in common. Heart and head don't always run in tandem.

The disjunction between political and cultural forms continues to run through the grain of so much contemporary socialist practice, with traditional political forms and processes increasingly left behind by the modernising and integrating processes of cultural and technological innovation. The meetings still apparently go on endlessly, the unreadable papers are still produced and stock-piled in bedroom wardrobes, the world of ideas is divided into 'correct' and 'incorrect' thinking, resolutions are passed, long-standing comrades finally get elected to the central committee, the 'people' are berated for their lack of revolutionary fervour, at the same time that popular cultural forms such as world music, jazz, literature, television and cinema recreate the world and our ways of thinking about it in potentially radical and encouraging ways.

This innovative and transforming political power of cultural forms and modes of cultural production I found described and persuasively analysed in the work of Raymond Williams, as was a whole new agenda for politics based on lived experience, the accents we spoke with, our educational displacement, our relationship with the particularities and social history of the landscape we lived in, the lives our parents and grand-parents lived, the newspapers we read, the films and television programmes we watched. But that came after I had left the world of the Young Socialists behind.

Andrzej Wajda's film *A Generation* for me provides the connection. For at some point in those formative years, one of our Young Socialist minibus trips took us to an art cinema in London's West End to see *A Generation* and some of us came home changed. For this film, coming from the other side of the Iron Curtain, moved and disturbed us in ways which the Western European and American cinema had mostly failed to do. Here was another kind of short-circuit, suddenly illuminating the dark night like the occasional blue arc-light produced by an electric train, enabling us to see through and beyond the conventional political understandings. We were simply one tiny band of young people uncertain about the future watching on the screen another such group confronting the same fears, though in horrendously more difficult and extreme circumstances. There were, we began to realise, no easy answers. A film from the East was saying something new and important about an aspect of our lives in the West.

A Generation is set in Warsaw during the Second World War at the time of the uprising in the Jewish ghetto, and concerns the rapid politicisation and induction of a group of young people into the Resistance, largely through the story of one young man. But it is not exclusively about life under the conditions of war. The early scenes portraying the routine life of a small working-class district, complete with pigeon lofts, outdoor card-games, pub life, children's street games, washing and cooking chores, bear remarkable similarities to the iconography and grammatical styles of a number of British social realist films of the same period. So also do the scenes showing the young man's first day at work and the culture of the workshop-cum-factory. The insight into the dilemmas of adolescence and the miseries of starting work, of being picked on and made fun of, was as fresh to us as anything we'd ever seen. *A Generation* is imbued with an understanding of the problems of young people that had rarely been explored in the cinema we knew, though Olmi's *Il posto* and Truffaut's *The 400 Blows*, both of which came to Britain about the same time, also took up these themes in very poignant and unsentimental ways.

The film also made a deep impact on us because the culture we lived in was in many ways still dominated by unresolved social and political issues arising out of the Second World War. The culture was awash with books about escaping from Colditz, novels and documentary histories of atrocities, films about submarines and Spitfires and upper-class heroes, and translated accounts of resistance movements in Europe. The civilian war in Britain, the war at home, which was very much the subject matter of documentary film-making and mythologising during the war, was very quickly marginalised afterwards, and the war of the many quickly became the war of The Few.

I have written elsewhere of this and I still feel very strongly that it is an area of cultural and political mythologising still largely unexplored. The pre-occupation with the 'settlement of 1945' has served to disguise what other social and political forces were set in motion during the war which consequently got buried and forgotten. It is sufficient here to say that our small band effortlessly and un-self-consciously elided the struggles of the European resistance movements with our own self-perceived struggles to bring about a revolution in Britain a decade or so later. We lived in dreams.

Seeing *A Generation* again after a gap of some 25 years or so, it still seems to me as powerful as ever, though I hadn't realised then how much self-projection clearly had gone on. It is a film of stark political choices, shot in highly contrasted black-and-white, full of shadows and images of prison bars and locked doors. Yet it has moments of unencumbered joy and delight in the physical world, and asserts the affirmative qualities of loyalty, comradeship and sexual love. It is a film that without qualification respects and sympathises with young people, a feature of much of Wajda's work.

That complicated and painful process of transition and discontinuity involved in the movement of power and authority from one generation to another, a key theme of Wajda's film, was also central to Raymond Williams's work. Certainly it is there in all of the novels, but particularly the first and second, the latter being titled *Second Generation*. Which other socialist thinker in our time has tried to understand the politics of generational conflict and change so thoroughly, seeing it as complex as class in its ability to stifle and divert existing energies as well as occasionally releasing them too? And generational change continues to exert a powerful influence on many 'structures of feeling' as can be seen, for example, in contemporary Black writing in Britain, or in the new cinema tradition of China's 'fifth generation'. I have always found it significant that Raymond Williams rarely seemed to be speaking to his own generation in his writings and political life, but always seemed to be addressing the issues of the generation following him. And like

Wajda's film and its main characters, he looked to the future rather than quarrelled interminably over the past.

In Williams's fictional writings there is the same painful honesty about community, generational conflict and change as is found in *A Generation*, and *Kanal* and *Ashes and Diamonds*, the subsequent two films of the early Wajda trilogy, and the same concern with understanding the pressures that test loyalties and sometimes lead to betrayal.

In the current breaking down of barriers between East and West in Europe, in the restructuring of political priorities to meet new problems and new dangers, cultural forms and understandings — poems, films, television programmes, novels — may exercise a key role in formulating the new, and asserting a different vision to the cramping and subordinating political systems of the old regimes. Williams's work has always resisted boundaries, crossed borders, and sought to find new ways of re-making the world. There are openings to the East again for a new political generation, and we should do everything we possibly can to make something new out of the decline and bankruptcy of the old systems. *A Generation* is an old film, but it is also, suddenly, a film for our rapidly changing times.

The Buddy Holly Story and the Popular

David Lusted

In Raymond Williams's call for a more democratic form of social organisation, a special place was held for the term 'popular'. Between the unequal power blocs of an economic system he held no truck with and the organised forces of working people's opposition with which he never lost faith, there was for him the abiding appeal of 'popular power', a living and potential force for social change residing in the everyday routines of ordinary working people.

On the side of the devils are the communications industries and the media, over which he sought wider and stronger means of democratic control and accountability. In *Communications*, published as long ago as 1962, he offers a programme to bring the media industries under popular control, a programme that remains as pertinent and as likely today.

Yet when he turned his attention to the products of those dominant institutions — the films, television programmes, newspapers, etc. — he made no simple assumption that there was any *necessary* association of meaning between the particular organisation of the media and the products they made.

Williams was tolerant of views one would expect him to consider outside his own political and personal commitments. His bearing made him open to learning from the opposition; immeasurably patient where others would lose their patience, willing to respond and contribute, to share platforms. In the same way, he was also open to the possibility for the genuinely popular to emerge from institutions he would nonetheless wish to be transformed. The principle was that it is hasty to assume an automatic connection between a producer and product, a cause and its effect, transmission and reception; for him, it was always more complicated than that.

By 'popular', here, he means more than that media products are indisputably received with favour by large numbers of people. A popular movement was one in which the active struggles for change of ordinary working people took notice of their social and cultural relationships and choices, in all their complexities and without pre-judgement. Ergo, the cultural routines of ordinary people, including their cultural preferences, were not to be easily dismissed. They needed careful, respectful attention.

Despite this, Williams infrequently attended to the centrally popular products of his time — his own preferences were for the popular culture (novels and plays especially) of earlier times and to recognisably artistic forms and political subjects — though his work on television light entertainment and drama in *Television, Technology and Cultural Form* licensed a new generation to new kinds of critical attention. The impulse and the opportunity to develop forms of criticism and apply them to quite unexpected, even trivial cultural objects were there in the principle.

Clearly, the implications of this line of enquiry immediately run into familiar problems, especially with the *very* popular. Think of a potential limit case. Large numbers of people read *The Sun* newspaper. Although there is wider sympathy perhaps for the idea that forms like the television soap opera or crime fiction connect in complex ways to the patterns of association and routine lives of the audiences who choose them, the case of *The Sun*, that most gross of insults to journalism, seems beyond retrieval.

I can't be sure how Williams would have responded here, but the great strength of his cultural work is that it opens up to scrutiny even the most 'no hope' of cases. A claim could indeed be made that even *The Sun* rhymes linguistic structures of everyday speech patterns, rhetorically sides with the powerless over the powerful, puts to work the personal knowledge and pleasures of its readership. And who is anyone to claim they can know the effects of a tabloid whose political affiliations are translated by a significant proportion of its

readership in quite contrary directions to any recognisably objective assessment? I don't know if Williams wrote about *The Sun* but I'm sure he would refuse the slur on its readership levelled by so many of his critical allies. (Even Jasper Carrot's otherwise welcome comic opposition attacks not so much *The Sun* as *The Sun*-readers, assuming their ignorance and passivity in a way Williams would certainly refuse.)

In the spirit of this argument, I select for the season an otherwise renegade choice of film. *The Buddy Holly Story* is a glorious example of notions of the popular, some of the more interesting prompted by Williams's position.

I doubt if Williams ever heard of the film or, probably, its hero — the two were of different generations, sub-cultures and commitments. But this need deter us little. The film's 'Holly' is not the Holly whose name he shares, who may or may not have displayed the kinds of racism and sexism the hero of the film actively opposes. This Holly lives just 90 minutes, considerably less even than the benightedly short life of the real rock'n'roller. The biographical details may well differ, events may occur selectively or be empirically incorrect; Buddy Holly may indeed, like Elvis, still be alive. I don't really know about these matters and it matters nothing — for my immediate purpose, at least.

The film's Buddy Holly is a character of fiction, one who works out in fantasy a utopian drama the rest of us live out only in our imaginations. The character connects to genuinely popular traditions of class and racial relationships, in opposition to oppressive, discriminatory and divisive forces. It does so, in the form of the romantic musical, where romance is a metaphor for personal and social commitments, and the musical its celebratory expression. In its content and form, it is immediately recognisable to its notional audiences. That recognition secures identifications between the fiction and its actual audiences, enabling fully popular argument and association to take place.

Also in its content and form, the film shares an interest in the subjects and problems that Williams addresses. And it does so in the same creative and provocative ways in which Williams addressed them, ways that alert so many differently-placed groups across so many social categories and generations, at times, not just to the good sense that is being spoken, but also to the sense that they are being spoken to quite directly.

The film commands the description 'popular' in two ways. It confronts immediate issues of how the past is to be understood for the present; here, how a period of cultural renaissance and new social aspirations in the 1950s and 60s is subsequently represented as idleness and degeneracy, a dominant reworking of the period that was as active at the time the film was made (1978) as it is today. Against these attempts to modernise a culture for today through archaic and authoritarian representations of the recent past, this film asserts with affection that that period, for all its faults, was better to live in than this.

There is an element of nostalgia in this, of course, but it is an active nostalgia, put to work politically in the cause of popular memory. For the film also uses history to speak about the present. Its concerns are those that confront most of us every day — how to live out our commitments to self and others around us; how to work for personal and collective changes in the interests of the many different groups we feel bound to by any number of social connections; how to deal with forces hostile to those intentions, indeed with more power than we to determine outcomes. In the film, the hero must negotiate antagonistic regimes among family, peer group, community leaders in order to establish a more genuine community among music-makers. The ideal alternative evokes a shared tradition, a 'structure of feeling', which actively inscribes social change, both personal and collective.

The film features a utopian celebration of the racial 'melting pot' with black and white singers breaking borders, physical (in the music theatres and ghetto hotels) and metaphorical (in Buddy's partnership with the two Crickets and then his wife), asserting the right of action against those who threaten the community (like the Nashville racist and the drummer's repellent 'dark meat' joke).

The film is also 'popular' in the way it speaks of general, ordinary conditions in commanding ways. The loving period detail of the film strengthens rather than inhibits continuities with earlier and later periods; centrally in the stress on place, from small town to big city, from 'decent and honest' homestead to slick offices; and in the connections with other times; in the black cultural history of the Apollo Theatre and segregated accommodation, and, comically, in the assertion of a common music tradition through references to quite other musicians like Beethoven before him and the Beatles after him.

But, as with Williams, continuities do not exist without struggle and it is in the drama to face and overcome conflicts, to transform relationships into rooted loyalties, that the audience becomes actively popular. The film seeks with its audience a complicity, an implicit call to share in a driving, burning commitment to overcome unequal power relations at a quite personal level. And the film, remarkably, does this in a compulsive way, putting its deep anger at injustices and inequalities into positive struggle for social change.

Williams's political anger was always contained, sometimes so contained as to make him seem more civil than his argument ever was, but it was palpable enough for those who share his outrage at the everyday, ritual barbarities of living that remain the lot of so many extraordinary people who must pass as ordinary and for whom 'power' is understood and experienced only negatively, as a right a few others take for granted to exercise over the many.

The film imaginatively reworks ideas of class connection and commitment, celebrating and extending these abstractions in quite concrete personal and social relationships. The hero overcomes those who represent constraints on these aspirations, changing or accommodating not just those outside his community who oppose his personal and collective aspirations (parents, disc-jockey, record company head) but also those within (the aunt, the Crickets, Maria Elena). In a comparable way, Williams was at pains to argue not just with the dominant forces but also among those regressive or neutralising forces within the 'broad church' of his own alliances.

******

Buddy Holly — *now*, the real one — and Raymond Williams connect for me as deeply formative and resonant names. Some years after the event, Williams's writing helped me to think through the experience of moving from one class to another through education in the post-War Britain of the 1950s and 60s. Buddy Holly's music was a promise of something better while I lived through it.

Holly's music, simple and affirmative, was an escape into colour from a relentlessly monochrome Britain of economic and social restriction. A few bars into the songs and the desire to make your own music took over. An evening of this kind of music and the monotony of school assembly hymns and squeeky-clean Light Programme tunes that stood for the passionless routine of the time receded. Elvis, the Everley Brothers and, above all, Holly, spoke of potential life, of romance and courage to a teenager with unfocused discontents and aspirations.

Years later, the associations linger. But while that white rock'n'roll led inexorably towards forms of earlier and especially black music that informed and transformed my sense of self, the songs that Williams sang led into a world of educational and political commitment that put to work my understanding of the lives on either side of the transformation.

Throughout the 1970s and 80s, in keeping with many others, his writing and teaching was a touchstone. A period of theoretical upheaval here or political crisis there would take me in other directions from time to time. But the sheer humanity and deep insight inscribed in Williams's products and, uniquely, even his public practices made my return to his latest work an inevitability.

I associate Buddy Holly with a feeling of fun, time out, making out, extending the affective side. But I associate Raymond Williams with a feeling of understanding and commitment. This film is most of all the site to reflect upon these connections — biographical, intellectual, affiliative. Holly and Williams, in their different realms of activity and thought, both helped me live. I'll not choose between them but I have to be grateful to Raymond Williams for making the essential connection so fundamental.

102

Z Cars & Pressure: TV and the Sense of an Ending

Charlie Ritchie

I first became aware of Raymond Williams on the TV; a fuzzy memory of two schoolboys watching a talk programme on 'advertising' one Friday night. The prevailing platitudes about The Horror Of It All were eventually disturbed by a single voice from the back. A Welshman with impressively long hair proposed that purging the forum's collective cultured angst obviously required a more fundamental political change than they had so far considered. Obviously...as we 'O'-level kids immediately agreed, but this was the first word of sense we had heard all night, and the image has prevailed: a patient but tenacious radicalism, cutting across the flow of 'informed' TV chatter, making the point that he had come there to make. In the couple of decades since, Williams's work in and on television has been a particular focus for my education, with his emphasis on the present and future possibilities of a popular medium always an inseparable element of his broader cultural analysis. Despite his virtual exclusion from the broadcasting centres of power, the voice from the back remains a critically optimistic one.

> We are now at one of those historical moments when the relations between communications technologies and social institutions are a matter not only for study and analysis but for a wide set of practical choices. (*Contact* 1981.)

Williams's arguments about audiences and cultural form have a longstanding affinity with the theatre and television work of John McGrath. McGrath's memorial lecture at Cambridge last year on Williams and Television emphasised how pertinent (and unfulfilled) the practical choices set out in *Communications* (1962) and *Television: Technology and Cultural Form* (1974) remain. When

Williams's *New Left Review* interviewers suggest he overestimates the possibilities of cinema and television, they cite McGrath's play *The Cheviot, the Stag and the Black, Black Oil*. He responds, 'I have been telling people all over Europe that *The Cheviot* is the most important recent play in Britain. I don't have to be persuaded of that. But I think it is a rather special case' (*Politics and Letters*, 1979). During the period of these interviews (which for all their extraordinary richness, do tend to underplay Williams on TV) McGrath himself was working on a televisual 'special case'.

Broadcast in 1978, *Pressure* is the final episode of *Z-Cars* and marks the end of one era in McGrath's career as television director. Thereafter, the political and formal innovation of *Once Upon a Union* (1977), with its unprecedented (and probably unrepeatable) collaboration of 'drama' and 'current affairs' departments, begins to move him beyond the BBC pale. *Pressure* is marked by the pressure of this movement, as McGrath and Troy Kennedy Martin reunite to kill off the series they had begun nearly two decades previously. Although this series has come to be seen as almost defining the strengths and limits of a particular type of television naturalism, if we view it in the terms offered by Williams's writing on television, further possibilities emerge.

Sometimes described as presenting crime stores from the policeman's viewpoint, the early episodes of *Z-Cars* actually offered different social settings and points of view (criminal, wife, child), albeit within the controlling frame of the series. This frame set the police up in a kind of ruse to enable a wider-ranging contemporary dramatisation of class, family, work and the law than the version of social reality put together by most prime-time TV. Episode twenty *People's Property* (1962) climaxes in an ironically beautiful pan around a Welsh hillside which holds out a vision of freedom shared momentarily by audience, police *and* the twelve-year-old delinquents they have been apprehending/identifying with. As the series ran, the pressure to centre on the popular figures of the police squad (James Ellis, Brian Blessed, Frank Windsor, Stratford Johns) exemplified Williams's general comment on police series in one of his *Listener*

104

columns: 'The almost irresistible suggestion, of these ordinary members of the crime squad, is that their way of looking at the world is the only available honest way.' The formal and ideological pressure here, then, is as much that of the *series* as 'naturalism' *per se*, and can be seen as a very specific dimension of the 'flow' Williams analyses in *Television*. Their continuity is '...not of an action, but of one or more characters... Certain formulas on which the continuity depends are then the limiting conventions within which they must work.' But equally Williams stresses that 'the cultural importance of the serial as an essentially new form ought not to be limited to this kind of traditional ratification. Few forms on television have the potential importance of the original series...their persistence and popularity is significant in a period in which in so much traditionally serious drama and fiction there has been a widespread withdrawal from general social experience.'

Pressure is a special case and offers an opportunity to see the limiting conventions of this particular series formula 'worked over', as McGrath and Kennedy Martin use the occasion of the series' cancellation to undermine the framing assumptions about police and society on which the series had come to trade. Thus licensed to kill, *Pressure* equally stages a bitterly comic assault on the series' (and the late 70s') 'withdrawal from general social experience', in a way that anticipates the ideologies and practices of the 80s.

Our favourite police station is undergoing a management crisis as increased powers and changing patterns of surveillance cut the squad off from the easy discourse of the community. Familiar series faces are cast in and against type, reproducing for the viewer this front desk confusion of identity and authority. The characteristic qualities of gritty probity and weary street-wisdom are under pressure and in retreat. The multi-strand narrative and 'dialogue' (to be fetishised in, for example *Hill St. Blues*) becomes a principle of baton-passing irresponsibility. A drunk called The Rhymer takes charge of the verbal signifier. He wanders outside broadcasting couplets and punctuating plot-lines, till he is stabbed in a pub toilet for his pains. Everybody knows something's up: they can smell it. The technology won't work. The main 'action' is the installation of a new security shutter (a precise contemporary reference) by a specialist who views the nearby tower blocks cooping up the locals as 'a security risk'. The station, in other words, acts out that stage of state technology that Williams identifies as 'mobile privatisation'. The series shuts up shop with the unforgettable image of the security shutter descending once and for all. Then even this 'sense of an ending' is comically subverted, post-credits.

Although clearly a *locus classicus* for the opposition of realist and deconstructive practice, viz. 'bringing down the shutters (literally) on one kind of realism and its view of the police', the programme also begins to gesture towards a third mode — the kind of historically precise dialogic carnival that McGrath's recent theatre is attempting.

Pressure can now be read in the light of the 'TV Careers' of both McGrath and Williams and their grasp of the contradictory possibilities of this popular medium as a social and political institution. *Pressure*'s attack on mobile privatisation reminds us how much of that '78 structure of feeling is still with us, how pressing the practical choices are...and suggests at least one sub-text. In 1970 Williams generalised in *The Listener* about police series' scriptwriters in the light of returning from 'the prison, where I had been visiting a student who got nine months...' Such scriptwriters, he noted '...seem extraordinarily preoccupied by questions of authority: who exactly takes the decision and gives the orders. Since the world they know best is presumably that of the television authorities, it is tempting to suppose that we are getting a series of objective correlatives of Television Centre. But I doubt that.'

For different reasons, in *Pressure*, I don't.

(With thanks to Sorley Macdonald, Cambridge Arts Cinema.)

The Herd (Sürü)

Tana Wollen

The bleakness of *The Herd*'s despair makes it an odd choice for a
season of films commemorating Raymond Williams's life and work,
for what one learns above all else from Williams is the futility of
pessimism. His commitment to investigation of a meticulous kind,
the sweep and strength of his analyses and the political resolve which
his writing held, behind the necessary questions it always posed,
were signs of a determined pressing on. Hope is never offered falsely
in Williams's writing, nor is giving up an option. What connections
can be drawn then, between a film which hammers loss and
ignorance into narrative and a range of work which urges intelligent
discovery?

At the end of the film Hamo, the old patriarch, is deserted and lost
in Ankara, the capital city of the nation in which he lives but does
not recognise. Until now the world has been one he governed,
according to the ancient laws of family and tribe, but the film shows
his grip loosening as changing circumstances force the limits of his
understanding. In *The Herd* the instincts of the oppressed are
reactionary. They can enjoy no neighbourhood, in that Shakespearean
sense to which Williams alerted us, but seek deliverance from threat
by attacking their own. The film opens with the rekindling of a feud
between the Halilans and the Veriskyans and, ironically, the source
of its tension this time is a marriage between the two. The Halilans'
sister, Berivan, had been given to a Veriskyan, Sivan. Berivan's
failure to produce children provokes a vengeful wrath in Hamo, her
father-in-law. He rails against her family, blames her for her
children's mortality and then mercilessly beats his own son for
daring to defend her, a mere wife. Fear and loathing in *The Herd*
bind kith and kin.

At first sight *The Herd* might be seen to dispel nostalgic rural myths — and there is nothing more pastoral than shepherds — in the same way that Williams begins *The Country and the City*:

> On the country has gathered the idea of a natural way of life: of peace, innocence, and simple virtue. On the city has gathered the idea of an achieved centre: of learning, communication, light. Powerful hostile associations have also developed: on the city as a place of noise, worldliness and ambition; on the country as a place of backwardness, ignorance, limitation.[1]

But to say that these myths of the country (and the city) are simply dispelled by Williams and by *The Herd* would be to simplify the connections they both make between the rural and the industrial, between individuals and their communities. For Williams goes on to examine shifting literary representations of the country as livelihood, and as a place where labour curses the workers. The country can be both experienced as 'unmediated nature - a physical awareness of trees, birds, the moving shapes of land' while its history can be made to reveal 'a working agriculture, in which much of the nature is in fact being produced.'[2]

The land which *The Herd* represents is as complex: like *The Country and the City*, the film eschews any simple juxtaposition between 'nature' and 'production'. The beauty of the hills is sharp, their colours as weathered as the people and livestock they barely sustain. *The Herd* exemplifies 'sheep eating the men' (a quotation Williams took from Thomas More), while the tractors, imported from the multi-nationals, turn the hillsides from grazing to arable.[3] As a landscape, and as the source of livelihood, this country's naturalism is edged into the symbolic. At the same time the film charts the beginnings of a migration from the rural to the industrial by people who have had their command of a limited agriculture wrenched from them. As Williams insisted, there's more to a socialist ecology than getting folksy and going back to the soil;

> Because of course these attitudes of mastering and conquering had from the beginning been associated not just with mastering the earth, or natural substances, or making water do what you wanted, but with pushing other people

around, with going wherever there were things which you wanted, and subjugating and conquering.[4]

If Williams has analysed British literary representations of the country, then *The Herd* is a cinematic representation of a very different country. Williams modestly acknowledged that his was 'always a limited enquiry: the country and the city within a single tradition', but it enables connections to be made with others, and for similarities and differences to be revealed. In representing a particular set of conditions in a changing culture, *The Herd* no more than hints at a political analysis, but the strength of its representations and the direction of its narrative call precisely for the kind of insight Williams articulated;

> There are discovered and discoverable reasons of a fully objective kind, for intense concern about the future of industrial civilisation and, beyond even that, about the future of the species and of the planet, under destructive forces that are already loose. But there are also discovered and discoverable reasons for a kind of hope which has long accepted the facts underlying these fears and which can see ways beyond them which are fully within our capacity.[5]

In very different political and cultural circumstances, *The Herd* develops a theme which is central to Williams's work: the crossing of borders. The nomads herd their flocks from the hills to the railway station because in order to reach the market, far-removed in the capital, they have to take the train. The train has been used to transport other goods - fertilisers and pesticides - and some of the sheep die from licking the carriages. Sivan takes Berivan with him in the hope of finding a cure for her in the city, but muter than an animal, her sickness will be exacerbated by drugs dumped, one presumes, by the First World. Sickness marks their journey across geographical and cultural boundaries.

By marrying Berivan, Sivan is a potential bridge across hostilities, and by challenging his father and trying to find a cure for his wife he begins to negotiate the tensions between change and continuity. It is Sivan who herds the flock across the country. For Sivan these are borders which loom at him from every horizon, and they simply have to be crossed, without him knowing how or why. In the end the borders have fenced him in: Berivan dies, the flock is worthless, enmities persist, his father is abandoned and he arrested. Williams, having made transitions consciously, would have recognised these borders which Sivan confronts as barriers;

> We can overcome division only by refusing to be divided. That is a personal decision but then a social action. I can only record what I have myself learned. Others will learn it quite differently. But I grew up, as I said, where the division was visible, in a land and then in a family. I moved from country to city, and now live and work in both. I learned, in many forms, the shapes of this history, its ideas and its images, in the society and the literature which had earliest and most thoroughly experienced a change that was to become universal, or at least offered a model for universal development. This left, in my mind, every kind of question and intricacy, and I had slowly to retrace the experience, in myself and in the record, as a way of gaining the present and the future through a different understanding of the shaping and fascinating past.[6]

Williams's autobiography courses through his writings on culture and politics, while it is measured by them too. Not only did he make a fiction of his life (as many writers do), but he pushed it to inform his thinking and turned his thought upon it, treating it as a symptom of deeper historical processes. Transitions were never uprootings. Communities and intellectual faiths were never abandoned but consistently re-worked and revalued so that the contemporary, and the future, could be apprehended in terms of 'discovered and discoverable reasons'.

If the calm and, it has to be admitted, often leaden tone of Williams's writing belies the pain and wrenching which his border crossings must have caused, *The Herd* lays before us experiences which beg discovery of their causes. Berivan and Sivan sit incongruous and incomprehending in the suburban cabaret. The film seems to be asking what these cultures are that clash and how they have arrived in these places. What cultures can these people claim? The old is inflexible and punitive, the new is tawdry. How can they understand the claims tradition makes on them in order to retrieve its strength while determining their own changes. If *The Herd* represents a loss of cultural value (and therefore the loss of political identity), in representing that loss so powerfully, it claims the need for a culture and a politics to provoke people into making their own historical discoveries and realising their own strength.

Speechless throughout the film, Berivan dies with her mouth open: oppression has overwhelmed articulation. Her refusal to undress for the doctor is not simply a naturalistic representation of religious modesty - the brightness of her clothes emphatically marks her negation. Silence and infertility amount to her resistance by refusal, but in the end this resistance is destructive as she turns oppression in upon herself. It's as though the 'discoverable' is too much for words and yet it is precisely the search for a voice to express which *The Herd* makes central. If the characters in the film cannot discover their voices, the film is itself the expression of how vital those voices are. *The Herd* not only represents a people's oppression, it demands to be representative of those people, to be watched as it speaks on their behalf.

In the range of his writing as novelist, critic and commentator, Williams's project can be seen as the unceasing effort to find a voice, to deliver experience to interpretation. *Keywords* still lives up to its title: a literally portable instrument to unlock meanings, for opening up confusion to clarification. Williams would never have claimed to speak for anyone else (although many of us claim him as an important representative of 'our' cultural politics), for his voice was one of many in many debates. The considered and qualified tone of his writing is not just one of the characteristics of his mental temperament, it indicates a particular intellectual and political engagement, licensed although critical. *The Herd's* declamatory force, even with silence at its centre, makes it a political expression of a very different kind, but one which would have met with Williams's recognition and agreement.

The duty to speak was a responsibility Williams never bore lightly. The speaking had a purpose - to discover the relations between culture and politics in order to strengthen an opposition to exploitative and demeaning relations. Those responsible for *The Herd* shared a similar purpose even though the conditions of their production were very different. Zeki Ökten directed the film on instructions from Yilmaz Güney who scripted it while serving a 24 year prison sentence. Güney escaped after ten years, but his films have been banned in Turkey and the Istanbul cinema which screened *The Herd* was bombed. The voice had to be found where it was forbidden, the expression forged beyond the barriers at great risk. Deprived of debates and influences, it's not surprising that *The Herd* almost bursts trying to say everything. What is remarkable about the film is that it makes reticence say so much.

NOTES

1. *The Country and the City*, Chatto and Windus, 1985, p.1.
2. *ibid*, p.3.
3. 'Socialism and Ecology' in *Resources of Hope*, Verso, 1989, p.213.
4. *ibid*, p.214.
5. *Towards 2000*, Pelican, 1985, p.5.
6. *The Country and the City*, p.306.

'Not Necessarily a Stranger and an Agent': Raymond Williams and Wim Wenders's Paris, Texas

Danielle Gardner

SCENE: *A man walks swiftly across a desert. A dust-covered figure set starkly off against the glaring sunlight. He climbs through a barbed wire fence, stumbles into a dark bar, grasps at some ice to wet his lips, passes out.*

SCENE: *A man and his son drive up to a junction.*

A pause.
The son asserts, 'Left, Dad.'
The father turns the car back towards Houston, his past and his future.

From sharp desert outback to deserted city landscape, Wim Wenders's *Paris, Texas* presents an apparently elegiac portrait of separation and boundary, of solitude and isolation. Successive roadblocks obstruct any movement towards community and communication. The film is fascinated with language and technology — the 'stumbling blocks of man's own making.'[1] Striking camera angles frame a land of speeding planes and trains, of cordless telephones and drives home from school, of space centres and electronic games, of looming concrete dinosaurs in truck-stop parking lots. An epic portrayal of 'the paradox of the communication of non-communication,' as Raymond Williams once defined the dead-end tradition of post-modernism.[2]

Yet this is not an Everyman tale of disconnection and dispersion, but rather a story of connection and communication, a lived experience of rediscovery and love.

> We live in a world in which the dominant mode of production and social relationships teaches, impresses, offers to make normal and even rigid, modes of detached, separated, external perception and action: modes of using and consuming rather than accepting and enjoying people and things...[What is important] is the perception and affirmation of a world in which one is not necessarily a stranger and an agent, but can be a member, a discoverer, in a shared source of life.... For we have really to look...at the real social processes of alienation, separation, externality, abstraction. And we have to do this not only critically, in the necessary history of rural and urban capitalism, but substantially, by affirming the experiences which in many millions of lives are discovered and rediscovered, very often under pressure: experiences of directness, connection, mutuality, sharing.[3]

******

The gaunt, worn figure of Travis walks out of the desert and into an alien and alienating world - the present/future wasteland which intellectuals commonly greet with what Raymond Williams called a 'physical shudder' of horror.[4] It is a journey out of the literal desert and into Jean Baudrillard's 'desertified' American city and freeway, into the sterile playground of mass communication and hypnotic images.

> All dwellings have something of the grave about them, but here the fake serenity is complete. The unspeakable house plants, lurking everywhere like the obsessive fear of death, the picture windows looking like Snow White's glass coffin, the clumps of pale, dwarf flowers stretched out in patches like sclerosis, the proliferation of technical gadgetry inside the house, beneath it, around it, like drips in an intensive care ward, the TV, stereo, and video which provide communication with the beyond, the car (or cars) that connect one up to that great shoppers' funeral parlour, the supermarket, and, lastly, the wife and children, as glowing symptoms of success...everything here testified to death having found its ideal home.[5]

In *America*, Baudrillard takes a quintessentially post-modern 'road trip' into the simulacrum that is America, into the 'giant hologram', into the 'fiction of America, the America as fiction'. His is a journey where miles and cities and people and space and energy amount to mere repetitions of themselves. No history, no future, just the frenetic buzz of the present 'hyperreality', of excessive and fascinating banality. By plane, by car, by foot, he criss-crosses a flat world of empty signs and functional gestures;

> And that smile everyone gives you as they pass, that friendly contraction of the jaws triggered by human warmth. It is the eternal smile of communication, the smile through which the child becomes aware of the presence of others, or struggles desperately with the problem of their presence. It is the equivalent of the primal scream of man alone in the world...This smile signified only the need to smile.... It is part of the general cryogenisation of emotions. It is, indeed, the smile the dead man will wear in his funeral home.[6]

Wenders ostensibly reproduces this funereal vision on celluloid. A phlegmatic camera places characters at the extreme edges of its frame. On a freeway, a madman screams evangelical messages to an oblivious audience of motorists. Travis's binoculars trace the path of an airplane's shadow across the lowlands of LA. The German doctor speaks in non-communicative riddles to Walt:

> 'Well, a lot can happen to a man in over four years...I guess...all kinds of trouble.'

> 'What do you mean?'

> 'Well - down here - a man can get himself into a fix sometimes and it costs a little to get him out.... You understand what I mean.'

> 'I don't understand you. I wish you'd get to the point because I'd like to see my brother.'

Travis chooses to sit in the back seat of the car, mute. The car's windshield reiterates the film's frame, the highway stretches out front, with only the back of Walt's head and the eyes of Travis in a rear-view mirror visible — an evocative image of the brother's simultaneous physical proximity and separation. 'Do you think he still loves her?...I think he does...But...that's only her in a movie...a long time ago, in a galaxy, far, far away'; Hunter segues fluidly from the memory of his mother to the jargon of Hollywood movies, from one (lived) image to another (manufactured) image.

SCENE: *A highway*

    HUNTER: (*in a voiceover*): Dad, if a guy put a baby down, travelled at the speed of light for an h— if he travelled at the speed of light —

Cut to: Hunter on the back of the pickup truck talking into the walkie-talkie, Travis holding the other walkie-talkie to his ear inside the cab of the pick-up truck.

    HUNTER: He would come back in an hour...he would be an hour older — but the little baby would be a very old man.

    TRAVIS: Oh. Yeah. How long would it take him to get to Houston?

    HUNTER: Ah..um..well...I'd say about three seconds.

    TRAVIS: Over...I didn't get that last part.

    HUNTER: It would take three seconds to get from California to Houston —

Cut to: Red neon motel sign of 'moving' horses legs.

    HUNTER: — on light speed.

The travelling twosome of father and son are divided by rear car window and walkie-talkie; horses — the symbol of the Old West — have re-emerged in the new west, literally at light speed (neon). Image has supplanted material reality: Muse Air airlines, 'I'm at my peak' billboards, drive-in banks, photographs of mail-order land. *Paris, Texas* seems to replicate the arena of 'a consumer society well on its way to consuming its own citizens...a society of destruction masquerading as progress.[7]

While Baudrillard's paradoxically invigorating road trip of death is obviously not the world of Raymond Williams, it is also not the world of *Paris, Texas*. The billboarded, freewayed, planed, trained and automobiled world of Travis, Walt, Hunter and Anne is not Baudrillard's frozen landscape of eternal self-referentiality. Baudrillard's sweeping generalisations are cracked by the particularities of Wenders's vision. Into Baudrillard's undifferentiated sea of premature grave-dwellers, a family comes into focus. Walt finally finds Travis walking the train tracks across the desert. 'Travis! Travis! Don't you recognize me? It's your brother, Walt.' At which Travis folds himself into the back seat of the car.

> There is at first an absence of ordinary connection and development.... but then as the action develops, unknown and unacknowledged relationships, profound and decisive connections, definite and committing recognitions and avowals are as it were forced into consciousness. These are the real and inevitable relationships and connections, the necessary recognitions and avowals of any human society. But they are of a kind that are obscured, complicated, mystified, by the sheer rush and noise of this new and complex social order.[8]

Raymond Williams's comments, here recounting the development of a Dickens novel, could be describing the motions and emotions of Travis and Hunter. The Dickens landscape of England, post-Industrial Revolution, with its monstrous and devouring cities, has become the landscape of America, post-Technological Revolution, with its absolute and enforced fragmentation by car, telephone, communication satellite, walkie-talkie — the incessantly sustaining 'drips in an intensive care ward'. Yet Williams and Wenders place an attenuated faith in an ability to override the determinism of the system, treading a line between the dominant hegemonic structures and human life as lived and experienced;

> However dominant a social system may be, the very meaning of its domination involves a limitation or selection of activities it covers, so that by definition it cannot exhaust all social experiences, which therefore always potentially contains space for alternative acts and alternative intentions which are not yet articulated as a social institution.[9]

Choice, alternatives, the 'irrepressible elements of authentic popular response', Williams's language is one of extension rather than limits, of connection rather than separation. In a tone that is very appealing in this post-structuralist age, he refuses to accept the determinism we are taught — the hegemonic determinism of the community and the technological determinism of communication.

> The basic assumption of technological determinism is that a new technology - a printing press of a communications satellite - 'emerges' from technical study or

117

experiment. It then changes the society or the sector into which it has 'emerged'. 'We' adapt to it, because it is the modern way.[10]

The Modern Way. The phrase hangs heavy with pessimism and inevitability. Technology, society's creation, becomes the actor; it limits, it controls the content of communication, the individual adapts. For the technological determinist, the myth of progress necessarily becomes the naturalised reality of alienation and division. The global village becomes a vapid landscape of sound bites, the reign of the nullity of Baudrillard's 'advertising smile'. Alternatively, Williams denies this inevitability, asserting that 'the moment of new technology is a moment of choice'.[11] 'We depend on certain "communication models", certain rules or conventions through which we can make contact. We can change these models when they become inadequate, or we can modify and extend them.'[12]

Travis, in his idiosyncratic manner, modifies. Almost all the communication that takes place in the film is 'media'ted — through telephones, walls, home movies, photographs, streets, cars, rear-view mirrors, peep-show booths. Yet mediation becomes medium. Travis and Hunter first communicate through the home movie, through an image of their shared experience. Later, in his magazine-inspired 'rich-father' look, Travis picks Hunter up from school. Walking on opposite sides of a winding street, Travis walks backwards, Hunter mimics him, Travis trips over a garbage can, Hunter playfully trips over an imaginary one. Finally, Travis crosses the road. Father and son walk off together over the hill. The drive home from school is transformed into an expressive walk. The rented Chevrolet becomes their car, the one with the dent in the hood. Billboards are received as art not advertisement. The dehumanising abstraction of technology is individualised, modified by and adjusted to personal experience. Travis stops the plane on the tarmac: 'I don't like to leave the ground.' There is a refusal to accept the modes of 'using and consuming...of alienation, separation, externality, abstraction.'

The 'reunion' of the family takes place under similar circumstances. Jane and Travis speak for the first time in years via the peep-show speaker phones, third person pronouns, and Travis's initial anonymity; through the one-way mirror; with their backs turned away from one another in their separate booths. Faced with a need to communicate, there is a fluidity and ingenuity in adapting the means available. As Travis turns away from the family he cannot be a part of, he explains himself to his son. The communication is mediated by time and space. But the film denies this separation as it flows from Travis speaking to Travis listening to Hunter speaking. The viewer feels the continuity of the communication — experiencing the soliloquy from beginning to end with both sides, sender and receiver, of the transmission.

The silhouetted figure of a man against a light-flooded window. There is a city outside the window, cars zip by. He is talking into a pocket tape recorder. 'Hunter, it's me. I was afraid of never being able to say the right words to you in person. So I'm trying to do it like this. When I first saw you this time at Walt's, I was hoping for all kinds of things. I was hoping to show you that I was your father. You showed me I was.'

Cut to the man, driving a car, listening to his recorded voice as the soliloquy continues.

Cut to his son, against the backdrop of a hotel room's large plate glass window, steel skyscrapers populate the world outside. The recorded voice continues. 'I love you. I love you more than my life.' *The boy holds the recorder up to his face, leans against the television, looks out the window.*

******

The voice of Raymond Williams was a voice of possibility and potential. A voice unwilling to accept the overwhelming pessimism that colours all that Jean Baudrillard sees. He did not celebrate the world he saw around him, but neither was he willing to see in it imminent and immanent defeat. His was not a career of formulas, or tried and true methods, but of readings and re-readings of traditions, of culture, of technology.

The institutions of cynicism, of denial and division will perhaps only be thrown down when they are recognised for what they are: the deposits of practical failures to live.... Nobody will be proud any longer to be separate, to deny, to ratify a personal failure in unconcern...[It is] a refusal to accept the creative capacities of life; a determination to limit and restrict the channels of growth; a habit of thinking, indeed, that the future has now to be determined by some ordinance in our own minds. We project our old images into the future, and take hold of ourselves and others to force energy towards that substantiation. [Yet] to know, even in part, any group of living processes, is to see and wonder at its extraordinary variety and complexity. To know, even in part, the life of man, is to see and wonder at its extraordinary fertility of value.... There are ideas, and ways of thinking, with the seeds of life in them, and there are others, perhaps deep in our minds, with the seeds of general death.[13]

Paris, Texas is a film of mixed genres and messages: the mythic American West, the radical estrangement of the individual, the fall-out from the technological revolution. In its unwillingness to accept dictated limits, it exhibits the spirit of Williams's articulations of choice, alternatives, and the '*creative* capacities of life'.

NOTES

1. Charles Dickens's *Dombey and Son*, as quoted in *The English Novel from Dickens to Lawrence*, Chatto and Windus, 1970.
2. 'Culture and Technology' in *Towards 2000*. Chatto and Windus/The Hogarth Press, 1983, p.141.
3. *The Country and the City*. Oxford University Press, 1973, p.298.
4. 'Culture and Technology' in *Towards 2000*. Chatto and Windus/The Hogarth Press, 1983, p.133.
5. Jean Baudrillard. *America*. (Trans.: Chris Turner) London: Verso, 1988, p.30.
6. *ibid.*, pp.33-34.
7. Wim Wenders as quoted in James Franklin's *New German Cinema: From Oberhausen to Hamburg*, Boston; Twayne Publishers, 1983.

8. *The English Novel from Dickens to Lawrence.* First edition: Chatto and Windus, 1970. Edition cited: Chatto & Windus, 1987, pp.32-3.

9. *Politics and Letters: Interviews with New Left Review.* Verso, 1981, p.252.

10. 'Culture and Technology' in *Towards 2000.* Chatto and Windus/The Hogarth Press, 1983, p.128.

11. *ibid.*, p.146.

12. *Communications.* First edition: Penguin Books, 1962. Edition cited: Penguin Books, 1979, p.11.

13. Raymond Williams. *Culture and Society: Coleridge to Orwell.* First edition: Chatto and Windus, 1958. Edition cited: The Hogarth Press, 1987, pp.334-8.

Credits for Films and Television Titles

GIVE US THIS DAY

Executive Producer	Rodney Wilson
Producer	Simon Hartog
Production Manager	Jim Pearse
Director/Screenplay	Phil Mulloy
Photography (Colour)	Clive Tickner
Editor	Charlie Ware
Art Director	Miranda Melville
Music	Michael Storey
Murals	Elizabeth Butler
Sound Recording	Malcolm Hirst
Narrator	Kate Crutchley

Cast

Robert Noonan	Frank Grimes
Bill	Andrew Boxer
Kathleen Noonan	Eva Griffith
Adelaide	Bernadette Mackenna
Mr. Sykes	John Dicks
Joe	John Joyce
Bert	Philip McGough
Mr. Burton	Nick Stringer
Old Tom	James Ottaway
Dan	Alan Ford
Fred	David Troughton
SDF Man	Bruce Alexander
Landlady	Liz Smith
Arthur	Leo Mackenna-James

1982	G.B.	Spectre Productions Ltd. For the Arts Council of Great Britain

LA MARSEILLAISE

Producers	C.G.T. (André Zwoboda)
	Marc Maurette
Director	Jean Renoir
Assistant Directors	Jacques Becker, Claude Renoir (nephew), Jean-Paul La Chanois, Claude Renoir (brother)
Scenario	Jean Renoir, with the assistance of Carl Koch, and M. & Mme. N. Martel-Dreyfus for the historical details
Photography	Jean Bourgoin, Alain Douarinou, Jean-Marie Maillols, Jean-Paul Alphen
Cameraman	Jean Louis
Editors	Marguerite Renoir, Marthe Huguet
Art Direction	Léon Barsacq, Georges Wakhévitch, Jean Perrier
Shadow Theatre	Lotte Reiniger
Music	Joseph Kosma, Sauveplane; Lalande, Grétry, Rameau, Mozart, Bach, Rouget de l'Isle
Sound	Joseph de Bretagne, Jean-Paul Alphen, J. Demede

Cast

The Court

Louis XVI	Pierre Renoir
Marie Antoinette	Lise Delamare
Picard, Louis XVI's Valet	Léon Larive
Le Rochefoucauld	William Aguet
Mme. de Lamballe	Elisa Ruis
Mme. Elisabeth	G. Lefébure

The Civil & Military Authorities

Roederer .... Louis Jouvet
Mayor of Village .... Jean Aquistapace
La Chesnaye .... Georges Spanelly
Dubouchage .... Pierre Nay
Leroux .... Edmond Castel

The Aristocrats

Saint-Laurent .... Aimé Clariond
Lord of Village .... Maurice Escande
Saint-Méry .... André Zibrol
Fougerolles .... Jean Aymé
Mme. de Saint-Laurent .... Irène Joachim

The Inhabitants of Marseille

Arnaud .... Andrex
Bonnier .... Edmond Ardisson
Moissant .... Jean-Louis Allibert
Questioner .... Jenny Hélia
Javel .... Paul Dulac
Ardisson .... Ferdinand Flament
A Marseille Leader .... Georges Péclet
A Marseille Leader .... Géo Dorlys
Captain Massugue .... Géo Lastry
The Drummer .... Adolphe Autran
Cuculière .... Alex Truchy

The People

Louison .... Nadia Sibirskaia
Cabri .... Edouard Delmont
Peasant Woman .... Séverine Lerczinska
The Curé .... Edmond Beauchamp
A Volunteer .... Gaston Modot

A Volunteer..............................Julian Carette
Bonnier's Mother ....Marthe Marty

and

Roger Pregor, Pierre Ferval, Fernand Bellan, Jean Boissemond, Pamela Stirling, Blanche Destournelles, Lucy Kieffer.

1938	France	Société de Production and d'Exploitation du Film LA MARSEILLAISE

THREE BROTHERS (Tre fratelli)

Producers   Georgio Nocella, Antonio Macri
Director   Francesco Rosi
Screenplay   Francesco Rosi
Based on the short story *The Third Son* by A. Platonov
Photography (Technicolor)   Pasqualino De Santis
Editor   Ruggero Matroianni
Art Director   Andrea Crisanti
Special Effects   Renato Agostini
Music   Piero Piccioni
Costumes   Gabriella Pesucci
Sound recordist   Mario Bramonti

Cast

Raffaele Giuranna ....Philippe Noiret
Donato Giuranna.......................Charles Vanel
Nicola Giuranna ....Michele Placido
Rocco Giuranna,
Young Donato...........................Vittorio Mezzogiorno
Raffael's Wife ....Andrea Ferreol
Giovanna ....Maddalena Crippa
Rosaria......................................Sara Tafuri
Marta, the Little Girl.................Marta Zoffoli
Raffaele's Friend.......................Tino Schipinzi

Young Donato's Wife	Simonetta Stefanelli
1st Judge	Pietro Biondi
2nd Judge	Ferdinando Greco
1st Friend at Bar	Accursio Di Leo
Raffaele's Son	Cosimo Milone
1st Friend at Bar	Luigi Infantino
Three Brothers' Old Mother	Gina Pontrelli
Nicola's Friend	Girolamo Marzano

1980   Italy/France   Iter Film (Rome) Gaumont (Paris)

DANIEL

Executive Producer	E L Doctorow, Sidney Lumet
Producer	Burtt Harris
Director	Sidney Lumet
Script	E L Doctorow
Based on his novel *The Book of Daniel*	
Photography (Technicolor)	Andrzej Bartkowiak
Editor	Peter C Frank
Production Designer	Philip Rosenberg
Traditional songs performed by	Paul Robeson
Additional Music	Bob James
Song *Give Peace a Chance* by	John Lennon, Paul McCartney
Costumes	Anna Hill Johnstone
Sound Editors	Maurice Schell, Peter Odabashian, Marjorie Deutsch
Sound Recording	Chris Newman

Cast

Daniel Isaacson	Timothy Hutton
Paul Isaacson	Mandy Patinkin
Rochelle Isaacson	Lindsay Crouse
Jacob Ascher	Edward Asner
Phyllis	Ellen Barkin
Frieda Stein	Julie Bovasso

127

Linda Mindish	Tovah Feldshuh
Selig Mindish	Joseph Leon
Fanny Ascher	Carmen Matthews
Mr Guglielmi	Norman Parker
Jack Fein	Lee Richardson
Robert Lewin	John Rubinstein
Dale	Colin Stinton
Lise Lewin	Maria Tucci
Rochelle's Mother	Rita Zohar
Young Daniel	Iain M Mitchell-Smtih
Young Susan	Jena Greco
Younger Daniel	Dael Cohen
Ben Cohen	Peter Friedman
Judge	Will Lee
Dr Duberstein	David Margulies
Funeral Director	George Axler
L A Receptionist	Lori Berhon
CCNY Student	Alexander Bernstein

1983   USA   World Film Services (US)
                                 For Paramount
                                 A John Heyman Production.

THIS SPORTING LIFE

Producer	Karel Reisz
Director	Lindsay Anderson
Assistant Director	Ted Sturgis
Script	David Storey, from his own novel
Photography	Denys Coop
Editor	Peter Taylor
Art Director	Alan Withy
Music composed by	Roberto Gerhard
Music conducted by	Jacques-Louis Monod
Sound	Chris Greenham

Cast

Frank Machin .... Richard Harris
Mrs Hammond .... Rachel Roberts
Weaver .... Alan Badel
Johnson .... William Hartnell
Maurice Braithwaite .... Colin Blakely
Mrs Weaver .... Vanda Godsell
Judith .... Anne Cunningham
Len Miller .... Jack Watson
Slomer .... Arthur Lowe
Wade .... Harry Markham
Jeff .... George Sewell
Phillips .... Leonard Rossiter
Mrs Farrer .... Katharine Parr
Lynda .... Bernadette Benson
Ian .... Andrew Nolan
Doctor .... Peter Duguid
Waiter .... Wallas Eaton
Head Waiter .... Anthony Woodruff
Riley .... Michael Logan
Hooker .... Murray Evans
Gower .... Tom Clegg
Trainer .... Ken Traill
Dentist .... Frank Windsor
Cameron .... John Gill

1963   G.B.   Independent Artists

BLUE SCAR

Producer   William MacQuitty
Director   Jill Craigie
Screenplay   Jill Craigie
Photography   Jo Jago
Editor   Kenneth Hume

Music	Grace Williams
Choirs	Port Talbot Afan Glee Society
Sound	R C Smith

Cast

Tom Thomas	Emrys Jones
Olwen Williams	Gwyneth Vaughan
Gwenneth Williams	Rachel Thomas
Ted Williams	Prysor Williams
Alfred Collins	Anthony Pendrell
Granny	Madeline Thomas
Dia Morgan, overman	Jack James
Mr Sharp, pit manager	Francis Lunt
Glenis Thomas-Evans	Dilys Jones
Thomas Williams	Kenneth Griffith
Wyn Jones	D L Davies
Mr Llewellyn	Winston Edwards
Owen Williams	Winston Edwards

1948   G.B.   British Lion

VALLEY OF SONG

Producer	Vaughan N Dean
Director	Gilbert Gunn
Script	Phil Park, Cliff Gordon
Based on the play *Choir Practice* by Cliff Gordon	
Photography	Lionel Banes
Editor	Richard Best
Art Director	Robert Jones
Music	Robert Gill
Choir	London Welsh Association Choral Society

Cast

Griffiths-Minister .... Mervyn Johns
Geraint Llewelyn........................ Clifford Evans
Lloyd-Undertaker .... Hugh Pryse
Mrs Lloyd-Undertaker .... Rachel Thomas
Cliff Lloyd-Booking Office ...... John Fraser
Davies-Shop .... Edward Evans
Mrs Davies-Shop........................ Betty Cooper
Olwen Davies-Shop .... Maureen Swanson
Bessie Lewis-Milk .... Rachel Roberts

1952   GB   A B P C

MS RHYMNEY VALLEY, 1985

Executive Producer   John Hefin
Producer   Ruth Caleb
Director   Kate Francis
Camera   Paul Reed, Roger Pugh Evans
Editor   Chris Lawrence

   tx BBC2 9pm 10/7/85

SO THAT YOU CAN LIVE

Director/Producer   Cinema Action
Photography (Colour)   Cinema Action
Editor   Cinema Action
Additional ideas and texts Chris Evans, Paul Willemen, Joy and
                            Raymond Williams
Music   Robert Wyatt & Scritti Politti
                            Alan Lewis & the Dulais Valley Sil-
                            ver Band, ar log II, Pig Bag, Lindsay
                            Cooper, Rui Simoes
Music Mixer   Ian Marlow
Dubbing Mixer   Richard King
Poster   Joao Botelho

Texts		*The Country and the City & The Fight for Manod* by Raymond Williams; *The Origins of the South Wales Miners Library* by Hywel Francis; *Politics and Letters* by Raymond Williams, with the *New Left Review*
GB	1981	British Film Institute Production Department/Cinema Action

FAME IS THE SPUR

Producer	John Boulting
Director	Roy Boulting
Screenplay	Nigel Balchin
Director of Photograph	Gunther Krampf
Film Editor	Richard Best
Art Director	John Howell
Music composed by	John Wooldridge
Costumes	Honoria Plesch
Sound Recordist	John Mitchell

Cast

The Boy Hamer	Anthony Wager
The Boy Ryerson	Brian Weske
The Boy Hannaway	Gerald Fox
Mrs Radshaw	Jean Shepherd
Grandpa	Guy Verney
Suddaby	Percy Walsh
Hamer Radshaw	Michael Redgrave
Ann	Rosamund John
Tom Hannaway	Bernard Miles
Arnold Ryerson	Hugh Burden
Lady Lettie	Carla Lehmann
Old Buck	Sir Seymour Hicks

Lord Liskeard	David Tomlinson
Aunt Lizzie	Marjorie Fielding
Dai	Charles Wood
Magistrate	Milton Rosmer
Pendleton	Wyle Watson

1947   G.B.   A Boulting Brothers Production

THE CORN IS GREEN

Executive Producer	Jack L Warner
Producer	Herman Shumlin
Director	Irving Rapper
Screenplay	Casey Robinson, Frank Cavett
From the stage play by Emlyn Williams	
Photography	Sol Polito
Editor	Frederick Richards
Art Director	Carl Jules Weyl
Music	Max Steiner

Cast

Miss Moffat	Bette Davis
Morgan Evans	John Dall
Bessie Watty	Joan Lorring
The Squire	Nigel Bruce
Mr Jones	Rhys Williams
Mrs Watty	Rosalind Ivan
Miss Ronberry	Mildred Dunnock
Will Davis	Arthur Shields
Sarah Pugh	Gwenyth Hughes
Old Tom	Thomas Louden
Idwal	Billy Roy
Llewellyn Powell	Brandon Hurst
Will Hughes	Tony Ellis
Glyn Thomas	Elliott Dare
John Owen	Leslie Vincent

Dai Evans ....Robert Cherry
Eddie...Ralph Cathey
The Groom ....Jock Watt
Gwilym Jones.............................Gene Ross
Rhys Norman ....Robert Regent
Tudor ....Jack Owen

1945   USA   Warner Bros.

THE TREE OF WOODEN CLOGS
(L'Albero degli zoccoli)

Production Supervisor   Giulio Mandelli
Director/Screenplay   Ermanno Olmi
Photography Editor   Ermanno Olmi
Art Director   Enrico Tovaglieri
Music   Johann Sebastian Bach
Organist   Fernando Germani
Sound Effects   Italo Cameracanna, Aldo Ciorba
Sound Recording   Amedeo Casati

Cast

Batisti..Luigi Ornaghi
Batistina, his wife......................Francesca Moriggi
Minek..Omar Brignoli
Tuni...Antonio Ferrari
Window Runk ....Teresa Brescianini
Grandpa Anselmo ....Giuseppe Brignoli
Peppino......................................Carlo Rota
Teresina ....Pasqualina Brolis
Pierino..Massimo Fratus
Annetta ....Francesca Villa
Bettina ....Maria Grazia Caroli
Finard...Battista Trevaini
Finarda, his wife.......................Giuseppina Sangaletti

Grandpa Finard	Lorenzo Pedroni
Usti	Felice Cervi
Seconde	Pierangelo Bertoli
Olga	Brunella Migliaccio
Brena	Giacomo Cavalleri
Brena's wife	Lorenza Frigeni
Maddelena	Lucia Pezzoli
Stefano	Franco Pilenga
Stefano's Father	Guglielmo Padoni
Stefano's Mother	Laura Locatelli
Don Carlo	Carmelo Silva
The Master	Mario Brignoli
Bailiff	Emilio Pedroni
Friki	Vittorio Capelli
Sister Maria	Francesca Bassurini
Sign Woman	Lina Ricci
With	The peasants and people of the Bergamo countryside

1978	Italy	RAI/Italnoleggio Cinematografico. A GPC (Milan) Production.

PAISÀ

Producer/Director	Roberto Rossellini
Scenario	Federico Fellini, Roberto Rossellini
From stories by	Victor Haines, Marcello Pagliero, Sergio Amidei, Federico Fellini, Roberto Rossellini, Vasco Pratolini
English Dialogue	Annalena Limentani
Photography	Otello Martelli
Editor	Eraldo Da Roma
Music	Renzo Rossellini

Cast

Sicily

Carmella .... Carmela Sazio
Robert .... Robert Van Loon
A Peasant .... Carlo Pisacane

Naples

The Negro Soldier .... Dots M. Johnson
The Little Boy .... Alfonsino Pasca

Rome

Maria .... Maria Michi
Gar .... Gar Moore

Florence

Harriet .... Harriet White
Massimo .... Renzo Avanzo
A Partisan .... Gigi Gori

Romagna

American Priest .... Bill Tubbs

Po

Dale .... Dale Edmonds
The Partisan .... Cigolani

and

Benjamin Emanuel, Allan Dan, Leonard Parrish, Mats Carlson, Merlin Hugo, Anthony La Penna, Harold Wagner, Lorena Berg, Carlo Pisacane.

1946   Italy   OFI, Foreign Film Production Inc., Capitani Film.

A GENERATION (Pokolenie)

Producer	Ignacy Taub
Director	Andrzej Wajda
Script	Bohdan Czeszko
Photography	Jerzy Lipman
Editor	Czeslaw Raniszewski
Art Director	Roman Mann
Music	Andrzej Markowski
Sound	Josef Koprowicz

Cast

Stach	Tadeusz Lomnicki
Dorota	Urszula Modrzynska
Jasio	Tadeusz JanCzar
Sekula	Janusz Paluszkiewicz
Jacek	Ryszard Kotas
Mundek	Roman Polanski

With

Zbigniew Cybulski, Ludwig Benoit, Jerzy Krasowski, Zofia Czerwinska and Stanislaw Milski

1954   Poland   Film Polski

THE BUDDY HOLLY STORY

Executive Producers	Edward Cohen, Fred Kuehnert
Producer	Freddy Bauer
Director	Steve Rash
Screenplay	Robert Gittler
Story	Alan Swyer

Based on *Buddy Holly His Life and Music* by John Coldrosen

Photography	Stevan Larner
Second Unit Photography	Alan Facemire
Editor	David Blewitt
Production Design	Joel Schiller

Special Effects	Robbie Knott
Music/Music Director	Joe Renzetti
Choreography	Maggie Rash
Sound Editor	Jerry Stanford
Sound Recording	Willie Burton

Cast

Buddy Holly	Gary Busey
Jesse Clarence	Don Stroud
Ray Bob Simmons	Charles Martin Smith
Ross Turner	Conrad Janis
Riley Randolph	William Jordan
Maria Elena Santiago	Maria Richwine
Cindy Lou	Amy Johnston
Sol Gittler	Dick O'Neil
'Madman Manouso'	Fred Travelena
Mrs Holly	Neva Patterson
Mr Holly	Arch Johnson
T.J.	John Goff
Mrs Santiago	Gloria Irizarry
Engineer Sam	Joe Berry
Preacher	Richard Kennedy
Wilson	Jim Beach
J.P. 'Big Bopper' Richardson	Gailard Sartain
Eddie Foster	Albert Popwell
Sam	Paul Mooney
Apollo M.C.	Freeman King
Luther	Stymie Beard
Avalon M.C.	M.G. Kelly
King Curtis	Craig White
Eddie Cochran	Jerry Zaremba
Ed Sullivan	Will Jordan

1978　　　　　USA　　　　Innovasions-ECA

Z CARS
Episode '*Pressure*'

Producer	Ron Craddock
Director	John McGrath
Written by	Troy Kennedy Martin
Production Designer	Susan Spence

Cast

Insp. Lynch	James Ellis
Sgt. Quilley	Douglas Fielding
Det Chief Supt. Watt	Frank Windsor
Chief Constable	John Phillips
PC Render	Allan O'Keefe
Sgt Chubb	Paul Stewart
Ferris	Tony Haygarth
Philpot	Gavin Richards
Det-Supt Boley	Alun Armstrong
Danny	Michael Gordon
Charlie	Chris Darwin
Red William	Philip Jackson
Maggi	Christine Hargreaves
Maguire	Neville Smith
Bus driver	Robert Putt
Girl at hostel	Julia North
Big John	Del Henney
Jim	Tom Georgeson
Tank Top	Kevin Lloyd
McGlin	Colm Meaner
Terry	John Gordon

1978	BBC

THE HERD (Sürü)

Director	Zeki Ökten
Script	Yilmaz Güney
Assistant Directors	Ali Özgentürk, Ali Kivircik
Photography (colour)	Izzet Akay
Assistant Photography	Can Ozer, Hüseyin Ererez
Editor	Özedemir Aritan
Art Direction	Rauf Ozangil, Sabri Aslankara
Music	Zülfü Livaneli
Sound	Tuncer Aydinoglu

Cast

Berivan ....Melike Demirag
Shivan...Tarik Akan
Hamo ....Tuncel Kutiz

With

Levent Inanir, Meral Niron, Erol Demiröz, Yaman Okay, Savas Yurttas, Fehmi Yasar, Göktürk Gemirezen, Suayip Aglig, Güler Ökten, Seuer Kökkaya

1978   Turkey   Güney Filmcilik

PARIS, TEXAS

Executive Producer	Chris Sievernich
Producer	Don Guest, Anatole Dauman
Director	Wim Wenders
Screenplay	Sam Shepard
Story Adaptation	L M Kit Carson
Photography	Robby Muller
Assistant Photography	Agnes Godard, Pim Tjujerman
Editor	Peter Przygodda
Assistant Editor	Anne Schnee
Art Director	Kate Altman
Music	Ry Cooder

Costumes	Birgitta Bjerke
Sound Editor	Dominique Auvray
Sound Recording	Jean-Paul Mugel
Sound Re-recording	Hartmut Eichgrun

Cast

Travis Anderson	Harry Dean Stanton
Walter R Anderson	Dean Stockwell
Anne Anderson	Aurore Clement
Hunter Anderson	Hunter Carson
Jane	Nastassja Kinski
Doctor Ulmer	Bernhard Wicki
Gas Station Attendant	Sam Berry
Car Rental Check	Claresie Mobley
Woman on TV	Viva Auder
Carmelita	Socorro Valdez
Hunter's Friend	Edward Fayton
Hunter, age 3	Justin Hogg
Screaming Man	Tom Farrell
"Slater"	John Lurie
"Stretch"	Jeni Vici
"Nurse Bibs"	Sally Norwell
Comedienne	Sharon Menzel
Rehearsing Band	The Mydolls

1984   West Germany/France   Road Movies Filmproduktion (West Berlin)/Argos Film (Paris). In association with Westdeutscher Rundfunk, Channel 4, Project Film

Raymond Williams - A Checklist of Appearances and Contributions to Film, TV and Radio

This checklist was originally compiled to support *A Tribute to Raymond Williams* which took place at the National Film Theatre on Saturday, 1st October, 1988.

The programme was as follows:

10.30 a.m.	Raw footage from *Making Shakespeare*
10.35	Introduction to the Day - David Lusted, BFI Education
10.40	The Work of Raymond Williams - Francis Mulhern, Middlesex Polytechnic
11.10	*Border Country*
12.00 p.m.	*The Country and the City*
1.00	Lunch
2.00	*The State and Society — In* (Orwell's) 1984
2.50	*Worker, Scholar & Citizen* (Extract)
3.00	*Identity Ascendant — The Home Counties* (Extract)
3.30 p.m.	Close

Details of screening on the day tribute

Making Shakespeare is a video currently being made by the Cambridge Alternative Video Group. It concerns the idea of Shakespeare and teaching the plays; differences in the conditions of reading and performing then and now. There are moments of interview with Williams where he talks about the Shakespeare audience, differences between oral and print culture, and the conventions of authority in television. The video is available for purchase for £20 from CAVG, 21 Cockcroft Place, Cambridge CB3 0HF.

Border Country is a programme made for the *One Pair of Eyes* series, transmitted (tx) BBC1 1/8/1970 (45 mins). Producer - Charles Wheeler, Director — Nicholas Garnham. The film is held by the BBC Archive and is unavailable for hire.

The Country and the City, A Film with Raymond Williams is the last of five programmes made for the *Where We Live Now* series, tx BBC2 23/2/79 (61 mins). The series, subtitled 'Five Writers Look at Our Surroundings', features individual accounts of architecture and the environment. Williams's contribution is distinguished from the others by the breadth of its cultural and historical analysis. The programme was produced and directed by Mike Dibb, edited by David Gladwell, with research by Helen Grygor and Joy Williams. BBC Archive; unavailable.

BBC2 transmitted a long discussion programme on the series on 24/2/79 but only the first part of it has been preserved in the BBC Archive, on VHS. In it, Christopher Booker talks on Corbusier and high rise systems buildings, Michael Frayn on suburbs, Colin Ward on new towns. Invited dignitaries, especially architects and their critics, respond. The preservation copy ends as Chairperson Brian Redhead turns to ask Williams for his contribution.... The tape is unavailable.

144

Identity Ascendant — The Home Counties is the sixth in a ten part series by HTV for Channel 4 called *The Divided Kingdom*. Kim Howells examines the triangle pointed by London, Oxford and Cambridge, guided throughout — but in person only at moments — by Williams. Julian Critchley responds. Tx 19/10/88 C4, 22/10/88 S4C.

The State and Society — in 1984 is a programme made by the Open University for course D209/1. *The State and Society*, first tx 4/2/84 (50 mins). Presented by Stuart Hall, it features several contributions by Williams in interview with Laurence Harris. The programme is produced and directed by Clive Holloway and Clifford Rose reads George Orwell.

Worker, Scholar and Citizen is a programme made by the Open University for course E353/2, *Society, Education and the State*, first tx 3/4/82 (25 mins). Williams is interviewed by presenter Roger Dale, with Heather Cathcart and Geoff Esland, all of the OU. Elsewhere in the programme, the then Minister for Education, Mark Carlisle, appears briefly. The first half, however, is devoted to an interview with Bogdan Fuchodolski. The programme is produced by Ken Little.

Other Contributions to OU Programmes

OU TV Broadcasts

The Widowing of Mrs. Holroyde (E263, *Language in Use*) 1981 - the D.H. Lawrence playlet is performed, briefly commented on by Williams, before Jack Shepherd reads the short story, written just before 1914.

Learning to Look, Asa Briggs contributes an Open Lecture which draws on *The Country and the City* in part, demonstrating the penetration of Williams's work, in adapted forms, into the mainstream of cultural and educational thinking.

Historical Data and Social Sciences, 1974 (no further information).

OU Radio Broadcasts

Industrialisation and Culture, 10/73
The Nature of 'Wuthering Heights', 1/73 & 1/82
City & Country, 3/7?
Language and Authority, 1/82
Further details and information on access can be obtained from
David Curry of the OU on 0908-655242.

Checklist of other Film & TV Contributions

D.H. Lawrence and the Culture Industry, Cambridge Alternative
Video Group (50 mins), places Lawrence and his critical reputation
historically. Williams features prominently, arguing a case for a
considerable re-reading of Lawrence that exceeds analyses in printed
publications. The tape can be purchased for £35 from CAVG, 21
Cockcroft Place, Cambridge CB3 0HF.

So That You Can Live, Cinema Action, 1982 (81 mins) is a 16mm
documentary about the relation between England and Wales, capital
and labour mining communities and industrial disputes, lived through
the changing fortunes of a South Wales family during the 1970s, and
in particular its mother, Shirley, to whom the film is dedicated. Williams's work is around the structure of the film, with direct
quotations from time to time. Available on hire from Cinema Action,
27 Winchester Road, London NW3 (01-586 2762) or the BFI Film
and Video Library 21 Stephen Street, London W1P 1PL (01-255
1444) for £35.

Raymond Williams — A Tribute, Large Door Productions for C4,
tx 28/2/88. A discussion on the occasion of Williams's death, chaired
by Anthony Barnett, between Dafydd Elis Thomas MP, Terry Eagleton, Stuart Hall and Judith Williamson. Produced by John Ellis —
directed by Don Coutts. U-matic tape unavailable for purchase or
hire.

Public Enquiry, BBC1 'Wednesday Play' tx 15/3/67, and *A Letter from the Country*, BBC tx 4/4/66 are two plays by Williams, the first directed by Gareth Davies and an imaginative reworking of Williams's relationship with his railway-signalman father. Both plays are sadly lost. The text of the first is published in *Stand* magazine No. 1; the text of the second in *Stand* No. 2.

A History of Nature is a programme in the *Crucible* Science series, produced by Mick Gold for Central TV and tx C4 16/1/83 (53 mins). Williams's *The Country and the City* is cited as reference, along with Carolyn Merchant's *The Death of Nature* and John Barrell's *The Dark Side of the Landscape*. The programme can be hired on 16mm film from Concord Films, 201 Felixstowe Road, Ipswich, Suffolk IP3 (0473-726012/715754). An article by Mick Gold based on the series appears in *Geography Matters*, Doreen Massey and John Allen (eds.), Cambridge University Press/OU Reader.

Big Words, Small Worlds, tx 22/11/87 C4, features Williams at points during this creative record of a conference at Strathclyde University in 1986, titled *The Linguistics of Writing*. A discussion between Williams and Jacques Derrida also exists on tape in non-transmission form. Enquiries about access should be made to Broken English, 10A Curzon Road, London N10 2RA (01-883 7946). Williams contributed to a book arising from the conference; *The Linguistics of Writing*, Nigel Fabb *et al.* (eds.), Manchester University Press, 1987.

Other untraced titles are *The Caucasian Chalk Circle*, an introduction to a schools broadcast 9/85 (?); a lecture in the series *Dawn University*, for Anglia TV during the 1960s (?); a contribution to a series on the press, chaired by Richard Hoggart, filmed in Birmingham during the 1960s.

Audio Cassettes

Tapes of lectures by Williams include:

— Thought Crimes, Barbican Pit, Debate 1984.

— The Writers' Forum, Cheltenham Festival, Debate 1983.

— Writing in the late 20th Century, Cheltenham, 1983.

For further details, contact Toby Oaks, Spoken Word Curator, National Sound Archive, 29 Exhibition Road, London SW7 2AS, (01-589 6603), for appointments to the listening service.

Raymond Williams - A Select Bibliography

Film

'British Film History: New Perspectives', in *British Cinema History*, edited by James Curran and Vincent Porter, Weidenfeld & Nicholson, 1983.

'Film and the Dramatic Tradition, in *Preface to Film*, by Williams and Michael Orrom, Film Drama Ltd., London, 1954.

On *Wild Strawberries*, Chapter 8 of *Drama in Performance*, Penguin, 1954, revised and extended 1968.

TV

'Culture and Technology' in *Towards 2000*, Penguin, 1983.

Television, Technology and Cultural Form, Fontana/Collins, 1974.

'A Lecture on Realism', about *The Big Flame* (Allen/Loach/Garnett) for BBC, in *Screen* magazine, Spring 1977.

Raymond Williams on Television: Selected Articles, reviews from *The Listener*, 1968/72, edited by Alan O'Connor, Routledge, 1989.

Culture

Culture + Society: 1780-1950, Chatto & Windus, 1958.

Keywords: A Vocabulary of Culture and Society, Fontana/Croom Helm, 1976, revised Flamingo, 1983.

Problems in Materialism and Culture, NLB, 1980.

Communications, Penguin, 1962, third edition 1976.

The Sociology of Culture, New York: Schocken Books, 1982.

The Arts Council: Politics + Policies, with C.B. Cox, Arts Council, 1981 (?)

For a more extensive bibliography of Williams's writing see *Resources of Hope*, Verso, 1989.